EMERGENCY

VIRGINIA GREER

Also by Virginia Greer
Give Them Their Dignity
The Glory Woods

EMERGENCY

the true story of a woman's
faith and service as
an emergency room volunteer

——◄◆►——

VIRGINIA GREER

——◄◆►——

CHRISTIAN HERALD BOOKS
Chappaqua, New York

To Ann Bennett, Helen Scarbrough and Winnie Smith

To Mrs. Cornelia McDuffie Turner, editor of the "Living Today" section of The Mobile Press Register, *for her encouragement when I was a reporter in her department.*

And to Mr. Winston Whitfield, administrator of Mobile General Hospital, now the University of South Alabama Medical Center.

Incidents have been altered to protect the privacy of the people involved.

PREFACE

A fashionably dressed woman had brought her maid's teenaged daughter to the Emergency Room of Mobile General Hospital. The girl had become ill at school, feverish with a violent headache. The woman, evidently kind and caring, appeared to be a busy clubwoman. She stood in the corridor outside one of the examining rooms where the girl lay on a stretcher awaiting the doctor.

The eleven other rooms were filled with patients awaiting emergency treatment. As a Pink Lady hospital volunteer, I was busy delivering supplies, a wrapped arm-board here, a vomit basin there, or noting a patient's temperature on a chart.

I passed by the waiting clubwoman frequently. Suddenly, she reached out, touched me on the shoulder and said: "I could never work in the Emergency Room. I have too much sympathy for people."

Her words seemed to hang in the air long after she departed. I couldn't get them out of my mind. They reminded me of what my friends had asked when they learned I was to be a hospital volunteer in the Emergency Room. "How can you bear to work in the Emergency Room? I couldn't stand to be around all those awful accident victims." These were reservations I had myself.

A day would come when these words would come rushing in on my own heart, and I would be faced with the dilemma of mastering my own fearful self.

But this book is a rebuttal to the nameless woman, an explanation to my friends, and an analysis for myself of what I was doing there.

It provides a glimpse into an Emergency Room as seen through the eyes of a Pink Lady, a non-medical volunteer.

I hope I will acquaint the curious with some of what goes on in an Emergency Room, but this book is composed with the larger hope that it may inspire others to drive with greater care; to be more watchful of children; and live with more lovingkindness. In short, to prevent medical emergencies from happening, preserving lives from the harrowing experiences of the Emergency Room.

ONE

I was brand new. It was my third day as a Pink Lady hospital volunteer. Ann Bennett, Director of Volunteers at Mobile General Hospital, had asked me to start the morning at the Admitting Desk. I was just beginning to feel comfortable in the strange, busy universe of the hospital. Just beginning to catch on to some of the simple tasks.

"After a while I will need you at Visitor Control, for visiting hours," she said. She was always busy, but always coping. She shook her head. "And I'm not sure whether the volunteer for the Emergency Room is coming in. But right now, go on to Admitting."

It was the last week in June. School was out and she was short-handed; many regular volunteers now had to stay at home with their children.

I went to the Admitting Desk and settled down for the routine. The first patient to come in was a small, frightened little blonde boy with a hare-lip. He had come for reconstructive surgery. Despite his wide, darting eyes, he was acting very brave. I escorted him first to the lab for a blood test. His father walked behind us. They were from out of town. The mother was not there, probably at home with other children.

As we walked down the hospital lobby toward the laboratory, I said "Your name is Joe, isn't it? You are such a big boy. And so good." He held my hand more tightly, saying nothing. I carried his admitting papers in my other hand, along with the lab requisition slip for his lab work.

I looked down at his dear little face. He looked up at me with his October blue eyes. Suddenly his eyes spoke imploringly to mine and a jolt of mother-longing hit me. In a split second I was going to be coping with tears.

In that endless moment I felt in that child's trusting face and hand the total of what I had lost. That portion of my life that was no more. There were no more children at home. Oh, I thought, how hard it is to let go. How we want to clutch and keep what was, forever. I got the shivers. The hand of God, I believed, had strangely brought me to this place.

I swallowed hard and blinked back my tears, because my loss should not affect his studied bravery. My footsteps quickened and we arrived at the lab. I told the solemn-faced little boy with his misshapen lip, "I'm going to find a toy for you. And this sweet lady will take your blood sample. I'll be right back."

From the volunteer toy box I found a little fire truck and a small book to give him. When I returned to the lab I had control of myself. The lab technician was finished, so I took the little boy and his father to his room, where a nurse took over. I waved as I left and said, "Bye, my little friend, Joe." Perhaps he did not speak because that would call attention to his deformity. But his silences were eloquent. They reassured even me.

I went to Visitor Control as Ann Bennett had asked me to do. I sat behind a desk, located near the elevators in the front lobby, and began inserting the patient visitor cards into the alphabetical flip-file.

A hospital guard was there. A tall, dark, friendly man. He was teaching me the procedure of admitting visitors and keeping records. Ann Bennett passed by and said, "It is so good to have you sitting there, smiling and gracious." And I did feel right in this spot. I felt orderly, capable and helpful. It was just what I expected my volunteer status would make me feel. All that was to change.

A few minutes later she came hurrying back to Visitor Control. "Virginia, they need you in the Emergency Room. They're rushed, with accidents and a D.O.A. But I need you more, *right now* in the Retiring Room." Her usually calm voice was strained. "There's a woman in there, Mrs. Campbell. Go there first, please. And hurry."

It happened so quickly: the Emergency Room, the woman in the Retiring Room. Had I really heard "D.O.A.," dead on arrival? The shorthand notation that masks the harsh reality.

I was so nervous, I did not know for sure why I was going to the Retiring Room, only that I was needed immediately. The guard took over the Visitor Control post until another volunteer could come.

The Retiring Room was a room with subdued lighting

15

and furniture in soft beige and brown tones. Families of accident victims, friends of critical patients, and most often the bereaved, could withdraw into this quiet haven and be spared becoming the object of curious eyes during their anguish.

The room was filled with people. Stark images of dejected forms, sitting. There had been an automobile accident. A man wearing a clerical collar was kneeling in prayer beside a woman who was weeping.

I stood just inside the door. When the prayer was ended, the minister went to a seat in the corner.

"Mrs. Campbell?" I said. The weeping woman looked up. I moved over toward her and said softly, "I've come to be with you."

I started to move a chair so I could be near her, when the man sitting next to her asked some inappropriate, unfeeling question of the minister. I was startled by his casualness. "Are you with this lady?" I asked him quietly.

"No," he said.

"Would you mind letting me sit there by her?" I asked.

He moved and I sat down. I put my arm around her shoulders and patted her very gently. "Could I get you some water?" I asked after a moment. "I'd be glad to."

"Yes, I'd like that," she said.

I hurried across the hall to the fountain, filled a paper cup and took it to her. I sat back down and put my arm around her shoulders.

She said tremulously, "I knew this would happen. But you're never prepared." She was still weeping quietly.

I could not say crassly, "What happened?" What could I say?

She said, "The emphysema was so bad he hasn't been able to speak to me since last Friday."

16

Emphysema. I knew how bad it could be. One of our neighbors was bedridden with it. Then I said hesitantly, hoping to learn something without intruding on her feelings, "How long have you been here?"

She said, "I just brought him over a little while ago." I still didn't know anything for certain.

"Is anyone coming to be with you?" I asked.

"Yes," she said. "My son."

She had placed the water cup on a nearby table. All the people sat and stared, or talked in intermittent bursts, exchanging reassurance, hope, comfort and grief.

The man who had moved for me was sitting near his minister, carrying on an extended monologue, which was really a prayer. It was about his son who had been in an accident and was in the Intensive Care Unit. "He's going to be all right because my wife said so. She's got a way of knowing these things. I don't know where she gets these things, but she knows."

I spoke softly to Mrs. Campbell. "Would you like me to get you some coffee?"

"Oh, could you?" she said eagerly and gratefully.

"I'll be right back," I told her.

I quickly poured coffee for her from the urn supplied for visitors by volunteers. When I stepped back into the Retiring Room, her son had just joined her. She was in deep conversation as she gazed intently into his face.

I handed her the coffee and excused myself, grateful I was no longer needed. She smiled at me absently. I left the room, hurried down the back hallway and pushed open one of the Emergency Room double doors.

Brenda, another volunteer, was already in the Emergency Room. "There's a little girl in Room Seven with a brain tumor. You might check on her," she said.

The door to the room was open when I entered to check for supplies. I did not know what to expect after hearing the words, ''brain tumor.'' Whatever it was that I might have expected, what I found was a pale-faced wisp of a girl of eleven, lying on the bed in pink cotton pajamas.

Her mother was standing beside the bed talking with her. A woman probably in her mid-to-late thirties, she was wearing a loose-fitting dress of material with blue and yellow flowers and touched with navy trim at the neck.

The girl's eyes earnestly sought those of her mother. She said in an increasingly loud voice, ''Mom, I don't care what they say, I've had all of that I can take. I can't stand any more of it. I can't stand it. Don't let them do it to me.''

As I walked into the room, she turned to stare at my intrusion. Her face showed no emotion, merely a steady stare.

''Hello,'' I said to her. I smiled.

Her mother returned my smile.

I said, ''I wonder if I could get something for her from our toy box, something she might like to have?''

I looked at the girl. She seemed to be looking me over to see what kind of hospital type I was. To guess what I had come to do to her.

Her mother said, ''Sally likes to read. She reads all the time.''

''What kind of books do you like, Sally?''

''I like mystery stories.''

''Let me see what I can find,'' I said.

Her blonde hair was clipped short. I did not know whether she had undergone a brain operation and had her head shaved or not. Her hair reminded me of Ingrid Bergman's in the movie, ''For Whom the Bell Tolls,'' grown out short-cropped after being shaved.

Unexpectedly, the box of toys kept in the Emergency Room was empty. Volunteers try to keep this, of all toy boxes, supplied. A quick toy or book placed in the hands of a child sometimes takes away the fear of the hospital strangeness. It alleviates the long waiting for a sister or brother, too.

I hurried down the long hallway to our volunteer supply room. It was filled with everything from garments and shoes to toiletries and a gamut of toys for infants on up to teens. And even games for adults.

Toy decisions are not minor decisions. To be successful, a toy has to be young enough or old enough for the child's ability. Only then can a child get some joy or comfort from it. If it is for a small child, a stuffed toy is good, but it must not have an eye or button that can be pulled off and swallowed. Even small decisions stalked us with their consequences.

I finally chose a pink plastic hand mirror and matching pink comb for Sally. I did not want to go back with only a book. Books are for lingering over and savoring. I wanted to give her something else too that she could use and that might please her.

I also searched deep into the huge box housing stuffed animals. There were cats, dogs, elephants, giraffes and way-out fantasy creatures.

For Sally, I selected a willowy long oddity, a pink-plush creature. It seemed the kind of something a thin blonde girl might like to play with, perhaps love. Then I selected a *Sue Barton* hardback mystery book.

When I walked back into the small examining room off the Emergency Room, I offered the mirror and comb, the cuddly, supple stuffed toy and mystery book to Sally. One by one she accepted them, no smile showing as she gazed

19

at me. I stood there. Her eyes were riveted on my face. Finally, she asked in a low, surpassingly eloquent tone:

"Are you the Play Lady?"

I felt that she was asking something extraordinary. She implied a warm magnificence in the title. "Are you the fairy godmother who makes wishes come true?" Moreover, I was a safe, reassuring person in the place full of people who must create some pain to heal.

I have never been quite as happy in such a special way as I was in that moment. I felt that suddenly, part of me belonged to her. She had a claim on me by her innocence and her need.

"Yes," I said, "I'm not sure exactly what a Play Lady is, but maybe I'm the Play Lady of the Emergency Room and didn't know it."

Her mother laughed. "When Sally was in the hospital in New Orleans, the Play Ladies supplied toys and played games with the children."

Sally viewed her face in the small mirror. It was a more relaxed face. She examined the boa-like toy and draped it across her legs. When she opened the book, I pressed her hand and left to go about other duties. Her mother followed me.

"Sally has a brain tumor," she said. "They discovered it in a hospital in New Orleans. Doctors operated and found it was an inoperable tumor. They gave her therapy for a long time and she responded." But there was no relief in her voice.

"She has had a remission for thirteen months and has been back in school leading a normal life. But the doctors told us it would flare up again, that symptoms would show up. Now they have, so we've brought her here because it is closer to home."

"I'm sorry," I said, "but I'm sure you'll get good treatment here."

"They are going to do a spinal tap now and that's what Sally was so upset about. She has had so much pain, she can't stand the thought of the spinal tap."

She sighed. "They have decided to give her an anesthetic to do the tap. I am so glad."

"I'm sure everything will be all right," I said. Every time I would say those words in the days and months to come, I said them as a prayer, knowing all things are in the hands of God.

She returned to her daughter's room.

Miss Scarbrough, Emergency Room Supervisor, came by as I was standing there.

"Tell me," I said, "the man with emphysema whose wife is in the Retiring Room. Campbell. What happened?"

Miss Scarbrough shook her head as she hurried by, and said in low tones, "He was the D.O.A."

TWO

Some days the tension and the hurry and the sorrow would catch up with me. *What am I doing in this hospital environment, spending six hours a day performing menial tasks, seeing sights I'd never witnessed before?* I'd wonder.

On my way home one afternoon almost drained of feeling because of exhaustion, I began thinking about the events that had brought me to this place and this work. It made me wonder at the remarkable turns our lives take. It made me appreciate again what an awesome thing we do when we ask God for guidance in prayer.

That's what I had asked for—new direction for my life.

It started one day, just two weeks earlier, I found myself in the company of two men in publishing. One was the editor of my first book. The other, also published by the same firm, was the chairman of the philosophy department of the University of South Alabama. Both were former ministers, Presbyterian and Baptist.

The book editor had come to our city on business and had invited the college professor and me to lunch. During lunch, between bites, we had talked at length about books.

"And what about you, Virginia?" asked the book editor. "What are you going to work on now?"

"I really don't know," I said. "Our youngest daughter has just left home to go to work in a distant city. I miss her so very much. There's a gap in my life now. There's nothing right now that I want to write. I am just staying home, keeping house. And reading a great deal. It has been on my mind, but you've asked me the hard question. And I don't have the answer."

After wishing God's blessing on each other, we parted, the three of us. And I drove home, still thinking about this gnawing need to be heading in some direction. I wanted to do something besides have a feeling of treading water. And feeling lonely in a newly empty house.

That night when I went to bed, my heart fretted with indirection. No tragedy was touching my life. Unless one can call tragedy the last child's departure from home. Sometimes we tend to see tragedy in what is simply life's natural process. And often I am caught up short, before I gain my equilibrium and remember that God's ways are higher ways, and we are in his master plan.

But I prayed deeply in my heart before my eyes shut and I drifted into sleep. It must have been about ten o'clock.

When we pray we are proving the existence of God. Not that prayer is a test—it is an affirmation. What an enormity prayer is in the life of a believer. Answers to prayers reveal

23

the reality of a God who hears. But often we are not prepared for what we receive as an answer.

I do not know how many hours had passed, but I awoke in the blackness of night. No moonlight casting its pale glow through blinds. No night light, tiny and gleaming faintly anywhere. I couldn't even see the luminous radium hands or numerals of the clock. There was total darkness and silence, but something had awakened me.

My eyes were open but couldn't distinguish any form in the room. I wasn't afraid. I knew my husband John was beside me. But I felt an emotion I cannot express. There seemed to be another presence in the room. I don't remember anything more, and I must have fallen back asleep.

I awoke the next morning and sunshine was teasing me into alertness. I lay still. What was it? What had happened? Then I remembered. The words: *Forget Thyself and Minister.* Had I dreamed them?

I felt at peace. I did not know how or why. And I could not bring myself to talk about it, not even to my darling husband. A few times in my life I had been strangely moved, strangely touched, I say by God. I had never known what else to call it. But never anything to equal the clarity of last night's message.

One week later on a Sunday afternoon I walked into the hospital, surrounded by the low-keyed chatter of church teenagers. We had come to tour Mobile General Hospital.

I was serving as substitute chaperone that afternoon for the 13 and 14-year-olds of the First Baptist Church of Mobile.

Peggy Haskins, the superintendent of the youth department had introduced me to the boys and girls.

"Some of you do not know Mrs. Greer. She used to work in this department with me. She has written a book about the teenagers who were here then."

She went on. "Mrs. Greer is going with us on our tour of Mobile General. Some of you can ride with her, some with me."

With my car full of the talkative youngsters, we began the short ride to the hospital. On the way I thought, "This is a strange way for me to see the new Mobile General Hospital for the first time. Touring it with a group of church teenagers."

My mind was rapidly telescoping. I remembered the old Mobile General. I had seen it for the first time in 1964. Its tall white columns splendid, but falling into elegant decay. The interior had all the sags and repairs of age. Its administrative, medical, and service staff, along with the building itself, were all hanging on for dear life.

For sixteen weeks in 1964, I had gone each week as a reporter for the *Mobile Press Register* to engage in intensive interview sessions with the administrator, Mr. Winston Whitfield, the director of nursing services and with other department heads.

Although I had lived in Mobile for over twenty years, it was the first time I had ever gone into the historic building which had been erected in 1830, and was a "tired old veteran of six wars." It was generally thought of as our charity hospital.

I was writing an in-depth series of newspaper stories that ran weekly as Sunday features for four months. The purpose was to explain the desperate plight of this aged Samaritan hospital which was in a financial struggle for its own life. We were trying to inform the public in an effort to

25

rally sufficient financial support to save the hospital.

During those once-a-week interview sessions, I came to know the old hospital, to understand its functions, its staff's personal relationships with the patients.

The next year, in October 1965, after five years reporting, I gave up my work as a newspaper reporter because of illness. After recuperating, I began and after a long while, completed my first book, *Give Them Their Dignity*, published in 1968, about the predecessors of this church youth group.

Since then the *new* Mobile General Hospital had been built with foundation and matching funds. The old hospital was vacated and closed. The new hospital had now been in use for over a year, and I had never been in it.

When we arrived, red-haired Mrs. Ann Bennett, at that time Director of Volunteers, led us on the tour. We walked down a corridor. Suddenly she halted the no-longer-talkative teenagers. It's always amazing how teenagers respond with sense and decorum to really serious situations.

"Ordinarily," she said, "we start a tour at the heart of the hospital, which is the Emergency Room. But we had a case of spinal meningitis come in there on Friday. So I won't take you in." She pointed. "That doorway and to the right, leads to the Emergency Room."

She turned to the left and pushed open a door. "This is the waiting room for Surgery, the Recovery Room, and the Intensive Care Unit."

Then again to the left, she directed us to the X-ray and laboratory departments. Leaving these areas we approached the front elevators. She pointed out the gift shop.

"Our Pink Lady volunteers operate this."

Across from the gift shop was the Visitor Control desk by the front elevators.

"Here are more of our Pink Lady volunteers," she said. "They issue passes to visitors and see that no unauthorized persons go up on floors."

Pink Ladies, I thought I had heard of them. But in my five years of reporting for the *Mobile Press Register* I had never done a story about them. I realized suddenly that I did not know their story. And it's one I thought that would explain the workings of a hospital in a way most people could relate to.

And again I was thinking of my own situation. Our youngest daughter gone. She'd been the last one at home, the other two children were married and living in far away states. I was missing her presence in our home so much. But more than that, I was overcome with a yearning to be of some real use somewhere. At the moment I did not want to go back into newspaper work. And housework consumed only a small portion of my time.

With Mrs. Bennett leading, we took elevators up to the Pediatrics floor. As we walked along the halls, she told us of the play room which the Pink Ladies had furnished for the children. Television, little tables and chairs, and games were situated around the room.

Small children wearing robes watched us. One sat in a wheel chair. One wore a patch over one eye. Mrs. Bennett smiled, patted this one, spoke to that one. She knew them all by name.

When we finished our tour and were once more on the

first floor, nearing Mrs. Bennett's office, I asked, "About your Pink Ladies—could you use me as a volunteer?" The words spilled out before I could stop them.

"Could I?" she said in obvious delight. "When could you come?"

"What about tomorrow?" I said. "Monday."

"Great!"

I hadn't even thought that this is what I wanted to do. And now it was said and agreed and it felt right. It seemed improbable that I, a normally timid person, would have volunteered for the job except for this chance tour. But then I thought of the prayer I had prayed and the words that I had heard. And I felt that this should be my ministry at this time. There was need and I was able. And I would be glad of a chance to forget myself for a while.

The next morning, a Monday, I drove into the front parking lot of Mobile General Hospital. I walked toward the modern monolithic structure rising twelve stories into the sweep of blue sky. The exterior was completely finished. On the inside, only six floors were completed and in use. The other floors were shelled-in and closed off. There was room to grow. Soon the seventh floor would be finished for a psychiatric ward.

The expanse of Mobile General's magnificent lobby of marble and stone greeted me. Switchboard operators were all but hidden behind the Information Desk, across from Admitting. The Medical Records Office to the right faced the windows of the Business Office.

Beyond and to the right, rising one floor was a curving stairway. It led to the mezzanine, to the cafeteria, and through branching doorways, to business and administration offices.

I walked toward Visitor Control, turned down the corridor to the right and went into Ann Bennett's office.

"Come and sit down," she said with a smile.

I did, and she began to talk about the volunteer program.

"You have come to help at the time when I need workers most. Many of my regulars can't come during the summer because they have children at home all day."

She asked, "Where would you like to work? Visitor Control? Admitting? Information? Gift Shop? Emergency Room?"

"Wherever you need me," I said.

"I know what I'll do. I'll make you a floater. That way I can use you where I need you the most. I'll give you an orientation myself. Today."

She looked at me intently. "How long can you stay today?"

"I'm free. All day if you need me."

"*Every day,*" I thought, remembering the silent house waiting for me.

"All right," she said, "First I'll put you on Information with another volunteer. Later I'll teach you Visitor Control. Then you can observe Admitting. And then you can have a shot at Emergency Room and see whether you want to work in there.

"Some do, some don't," she continued. "Many volunteers want Emergency Room. That's where the real action is."

She paused. "It takes a certain quality in volunteers though for the Emergency Room. Unexpected situations put you on your initiative."

29

With Ann Bennett as my teacher, I learned that each service had its complexities. At the Information Desk, I was taught to answer questions carefully over the phone regarding ill and critical patients and to keep the roster up-to-date on admissions.

At Visitor Control you had to exercise discreet tact. The situations that arise are almost unimaginable. If a patient with a second wife does not want to be visited by his first wife, you have to be diplomatic. It rapidly became clear to me that a volunteer had to be on her toes, no matter which station she served.

Over an early lunch, Ann Bennett asked me also if I would be willing to write a column for the little hospital newspaper, a column about volunteer activities.

"I'd be glad to," I said. I welcomed the discipline of a specific writing assignment. And I hoped this would start me working more on writing again.

Then she said, "Let's go to the Emergency Room." We did, and there she re-introduced me to Miss Helen Scarbrough, R.N., Emergency Room Supervisor. Helen and I had first met when I was writing the newspaper series on the old hospital.

"Yes," said Miss Scarbrough, "I remember Mrs. Greer." She seemed happy to have another volunteer. She escorted me around the Emergency Room on a personal tour before I began my on-the-scene training.

When I had visited the old hospital's Emergency Room as a journalist, I had noted the staff and the patients and their situations. I had not known what volunteers did there.

Miss Scarbrough showed her pride in the new facilities. She led me past the twelve examining rooms, with a look into each one.

The first thing I noticed right off was that each room had a door. A handsome heavy door with a push panel from the outside and a pull handle on the inside. The old Mobile General Emergency Room had fewer, smaller examining rooms which had only had green pull curtains made of the same kind of green cotton cloth used in those baggy uniforms worn by operating room personnel.

Patients in pain could have more privacy now. It was a simple mark of progress that showed the hospital's improvement and concern.

As Miss Scarbrough showed me the examining rooms and their emergency equipment, there were only a few patients in sight. I spent the rest of that day with another volunteer, observing and learning to do, by doing. I thought, "I will never learn it all."

But I discovered I'm a fast study, and I did learn the maze-like directions to the Laboratory, what supplies needed to be restocked and when, and how to fold sheets and make beds, emergency-room style.

When I walked out of the hospital late that first afternoon, I was tired and full of new knowledge. I did not know how much more bone-weary and knowledgeable I would become in a very short while. But I thanked God for the opportunity of service.

THREE

After my introduction to the Emergency Room and its realm of despair, hope and dramatic intensity, I found myself being assigned there on a regular basis.

Soon I learned there was a steady rhythm you have to pick up in order to serve at peak efficiency and keep your emotions in balance. Work in a hospital starts with cleaning and ends with it. When a room was emptied an R.N. (Registered Nurse) would call, "Mrs. Greer, would you get Room Six or Nine (or whatever the number) ready."

I would go in with a linen cart, remove the dirty sheets, place fresh linen on the stretcher bed. I would gather up everything left or used in the room, any used supplies and deposit them in the "dirty room" located at the rear of the Emergency Room complex for that purpose. I would then turn off the light in the examining room and leave the door open. A darkened room, an open door indicated that it was ready for a new patient.

It was a rainy morning. Outside was totally gray. The rain and fog made the air unpleasant and thick as soup. And you can count on smash-ups on the highway on such a morning.

The Emergency Room was already in high gear. The twelve rooms were filling rapidly. The dreary weather seemed to compound the atmosphere inside.

A sixteen-year-old boy lay on the bed in one room. His leg was lacerated. A yellow motorcycle helmet rested on a stool. He was watching the door eagerly, looking at the activity.

"You ride a motor?" I asked, indicating his helmet.

"Yes, Ma'am," he said. "That helmet saved my life."

I said to him, "My son rode a motorcycle during high school and college. He races them now as a hobby on weekends. I'm glad to see that you wear a helmet." I scanned the room quickly for supplies needed, then waved goodbye.

The next room housed an asthma patient. She lay on a bed, breathing from the inhalator which was attached to a long hose connected to the supply of oxygen.

A woman in the next room had high blood pressure, a condition as prevalent as asthma. Both sorts of patients came with steady frequency to the Emergency Room. It often led me to wonder about our environment, the one around us and the one inside us. What a world of pollution and tension we have created for ourselves.

OB's were in the next two rooms. These are the obstetric patients. They arrive even more regularly than the asthmatics and high blood pressure patients.

If a door were closed, and I did not know what type of patient was inside, I always asked someone before I entered. This time I asked Miss Scarbrough about Room Six.

"Oh," she said. "There's an auto accident in there, a teenaged boy. You can go in to check for supplies. But so you won't go into shock, I'll tell you that he has a gearshift sticking out of his chest." I must have blanched, but she spoke casually so I trusted that the case was not critical. Still I gulped hard before I entered that doorway.

There he was, lying with a short gearshift protruding out of his collar bone. He was fully conscious, apparently in no pain. They had brought the portable X-ray to him, and he was soon to go to surgery for removal of the stick.

I smiled at him; he grinned back. I said, "That's a wicked looking thing you've got there."

"Yep," he said, "after they take it out, I want to keep it for a souvenir."

I could sense his odd masculine pride at the prospects of displaying the object at a later date. He would be a big man to have survived that ordeal. His trophy would be the proof. Perhaps it would make him think about driving more carefully, too.

Then he said, "Would you tell me about my mother? Is she all right? I know she's worrying about me. Will you tell her that I'm all right? I wish I could see her."

I went immediately to locate his mother. She was in Room Eight. She had been uninjured in the accident. But she was badly shaken. I reassured her that her son was fine. "He's in there worrying about you," I said.

"I'm all right," she said, "but I'm so upset about him.

The nurse and doctor both told me he's going to be fine, but I'm still worried. When I saw him with that . . . thing . . . I . . ."

"He's all right," I said. "He's joking about it. But now what each of you must do is to stop worrying about the other one."

I walked toward the door. "I'll go back and tell him that you are fine so he won't worry either." I popped in and gave him the message.

My teenage friend with the gearshift was lucky. He lived to tell his Believe-It-Or-Not tale.

But, over 55,000 people in America that year did not live to tell about it. Over 1,000 a week. Due to drinking, speeding, recklessness, and the maddening and wearying rush of our daily lives.

These figures given by the National Safety Council have no reality as digits. But as people, as humans, the statistics take on a monstrous reality.

This does not include the two million people who received disabling injuries a year, nor the two million who received lesser injuries. Nor do the figures describe the toll on their families.

As a Pink Lady in the Emergency Room, I saw so many automobile accident patients brought in that I became fearful of getting into my own car to drive. I learned to drive with more concentration and care.

I witnessed the unendurable agony of the critically injured. I viewed the helpless anguish of their loved ones. Some memories I keep pushed deep within me. But they are there, because the automobile accidents keep happening. Once while I was there, a whole family was brought in—father, mother, girl five, boy three, and a nine-month-old infant. Only the mother survived.

Doctors, nurses, aides and orderlies were extremely busy in the different rooms. As I entered each room, my eyes roamed, checking my mental list. I replenished sheets and gowns when they were low in the cabinets.

In Room Nine there was a small child who had just been rushed in, gagging blood. He had swallowed a solution from a soft drink bottle which he'd found behind a neighbor's refrigerator. The bottle held some kind of cleaning solution which a relative of the neighbor had poured into the soft drink bottle and carelessly left there. It made me feel again the precarious condition of childhood, and remember my fears about allowing my own children the simple freedom to roam about and grow as all children must.

His parents had wisely brought in the bottle. Now the doctors and nurses were pulled into action trying to determine what it was that the child had swallowed. With no label, and no certainty as to what the liquid was, the urgent problem was to determine what antidote to use. A quick call was sent for milk, but no definite treatment would begin until specific knowledge was attained.

Reminding people about being cautious in order to avoid accidents may be as near futile as warning people to avoid pride or sin—yet the plea must be made constantly.

I continued bed-making and when all the rooms were either filled with patients or waiting to be filled, I began folding the sheets that had arrived from the laundry. They had to be more compactly folded in order to fit into the room cabinets. It was odd to be on the periphery of such vital activity, a necessary but not a crucial part—see and feel all that was happening, and have so little control over it.

Finally, the little boy who had swallowed the cleaning solution was being attended. They had made a determination of the contents, and now he would be admitted to the hospital for treatment and careful observation.

The asthmatics who had arrived before I did, were refreshed and breathing more easily. Some were soon to be released. As the stretcher bed in a room was made ready, another patient was brought in from what seemed an unending and inexhaustible number of tragedies in the world outside.

I picked up paper cups containing specimens sitting on the counter top located at the front of the Emergency Room and rushed them to the lab. Behind this counter and below it, was a long low desk at which the doctors sat, writing on the patients' charts or poring over medical books, drug lists and other reports.

When I returned from the lab, the boy with the protruding gearshift was being wheeled to surgery. The youth with the lacerated leg from the motorcycle accident had been treated and released, thankful for his helmet and his life.

Hours later I passed the room where Sally had been. The door was open, so I realized that the room was empty. It had just been vacated. The bed was still rumpled, the comical fuzzy toy was on the table; the book, mirror and comb were on the sink counter. I looked around and found that her mother was just wheeling Sally out to their car in a wheelchair.

I grabbed up the abandoned items, ran and caught up with them. I helped Sally's mother get her into the car.

Sally was whimpering at the pain of moving. When she was situated on the back seat, I picked up the book, soft toy and mirror-comb set which I'd placed on the hood of the car.

I said, "Here are your things. You forgot them."

"We weren't sure she was supposed to take them home," her mother said.

"Yes, these belong to Sally," I said.

"Thank you so much," the woman answered. Sally tried to smile through lips pressed tight with pain. Her mother closed the door as gently as she could, and started the motor. I stood there and waved goodbye.

The car windows were open and her mother said, "Tell your Play Lady goodbye, Sally."

From the back seat where she was lying, Sally smiled a feeble smile and waved weakly. I felt as if I had been hugged by her. They drove away as I stood there waving.

I stood there in the wide expanse of the Emergency Room entrance area. And I thought of the kaleidoscopic happenings, events giving way, moving on, making way for other small flash-floods of human drama, life and death. That was the Emergency Room.

Could I go back into that Emergency Room? I knew what would lie ahead for me. The torment I would feel for others, the helplessness.

If I had not known that God was working his own way with that pale eleven-year-old girl with the brain tumor, and with me, and all the others, I could not have returned.

But I did.

FOUR

Every time I hear a siren or learn of fire or disaster, my mind visualizes the Emergency Room receiving the victims and moving into action.

Once you work in a hospital, a siren is no longer an anonymous wail in the distance. It becomes personal to you. You become starkly aware of the harsh realities of life, and the tragedies that come to even the quietest, nicest suburb.

I was beginning my second week, putting in five days a week, six hours a day.

I hurried into the hospital that morning as I did each morning; I was always conscious that my footsteps were rushing me toward a paradoxically impersonal world which had a great personal effect on me—on everyone who enters this border land between life and death. Yet for me the image of the place was not an embattled border-land, but a realm over which the presence of God hovered like a comforting dove.

I signed in the hours' book, chatted a moment with Ann Bennett, now my friend. She had assigned me to permanent work in the Emergency Room. I greeted the E.R. Admitting Clerk with a wave and a smile. And then after walking through a couple of doorways, I entered the rear side of the Admitting Desk area.

Quickly I slipped my summer suit jacket off. I thrust my arms into my Pink Lady smock, onto which I had sewn the hospital auxiliary circular insignia which was embroidered in white, blue, gold and red. I buttoned my smock as I stepped out of my dress shoes and into my rubber soled white slip-on canvas shoes. I always felt like Mary Poppins when I went bouncing down the hallways in them.

Dressed now, I looked for Miss Scarbrough to get my instructions in case she had any specific chores for me. Or I would begin checking rooms for needed supplies.

I saw the Supervisor in a corner of the Emergency Room. Her back was to me, but I could see that she had a handkerchief to her face.

A young nurse, Miss Sarasen, pulled me aside and said softly, "Mrs. Greer, would you like to help me?"

I murmured, "Yes, of course."

As we approached one of the rooms, she said, "Mrs. Greer, have you ever seen a body?"

It was an unexpected question. And I felt a dread that I had repressed rise in me. Yet, I must have known I'd have to face it sometime. The very name, Emergency Room, conjures up confrontation with death. But I hadn't come face to face with death these first two weeks while learning

40

the intricacies of the place. Now this came almost as a test after basic preparation.

Of course I'd been to a funeral parlor, but I knew this would be different. More immediate. One came upon death suddenly here and the mind had no time to prepare for it.

She pushed open the door. "Oh, my. This is it," I thought.

Inside, two young men lay on stretchers. They were dead. One looked to be in his mid-twenties. The age of my son. "They drowned," the aide said. "We need to supply the room for the doctors."

I would discover many times over that "This is it" feeling. And every time it would be different. And the same. I never became accustomed to it. A gasp and a long emotional roller coaster plunge.

Next Miss Sarasen said softly, "A woman in the next room was brought in, a heart attack. They couldn't save her. She died a few minutes ago."

She added, "You probably saw Miss Scarbrough out there. No matter how often it happens, she cares so much that a death always affects her. Now she has to tell the grown daughter of the woman that her mother is dead."

Not one encounter with death—but three inside a few minutes' span. I was learning of the intensity with which the life and death drama touches those who served here.

I did not know that before long all of it would take its emotional toll on me.

What had an equal effect on me in those first days was the sheer amount of energy expended in the task. Especially for a woman who had not in many years put in such energy-demanding hours. I walked seemingly hundreds of miles at a brisk pace. The Emergency Room I found is no place for someone who wants to appear as a noble lady wearing a pink frock.

Many of the tasks are menial, some of them dirty. I learned a thousand simple tasks where I could be of service. That was the key. I helped people in need who were being ministered to by doctors and nurses and aides and orderlies and even me.

My legs protested and ached from running errands. My arms got tired from stacking sheets and linens for the cabinets and putting in medicines.

Newly-discovered muscles in my shoulders ached from all the hurried stretcher-bed making. As one patient was released, the next waiting patient must have a clean bed on which to be examined. I was beginning to lose my appreciation for fresh white sheets.

One day after lunch when I returned to the Emergency Room, a thin elderly woman was sitting on the side of the bed in Room Ten. Her right hand was soaking in a small basin of sterile water containing an antiseptic solution.

I smiled at her and went on my way. She was the only person in the Emergency Room at that moment. It was eerily quiet. You could have sliced the silence it was so solid.

"This is weird," I said to a nurses' aide. "I didn't know it ever got this quiet. There is only one patient in the place."

"Shhhh," she almost shouted. "Don't *say* that out loud, Mrs. Greer. You'll put your mouth on the quiet, then everything will break loose. Quiet is one thing you never mention in here."

I learned that there were "stage superstitions" in the Emergency Room. Well, I thought if the quiet might not be commented on, it certainly could be taken advantage of. I took a moment to relax and then caught up on tasks that often had to be accomplished in the whirling rush of emergencies.

I wrapped arm boards with cotton gauze so a supply of them would be handy when demanded. These are the thin wooden splints used to steady the arm for intravenous solutions, blood, glucose, and for bracing fractured limbs. Miss Scarbrough and the other R.N.'s, and even on occasion an intern or two, were generous in showing me a few techniques.

The Supervisor had once said, "During the times when we aren't busy I'll teach you to do different things. Then when we are rushed you can be of great help with some of the jobs that slow us down."

She now asked me, "Mrs. Greer, has anyone ever showed you how to do a suture set-up?"

"No, Ma'am," I said. "What's a suture set-up?"

She explained by leading me to the large supply room in the center of the Emergency Room complex. She reached for a linen-wrapped square "something" on a high shelf, took it and said, "Let's go in a room and I'll show you."

Since there were no new patients to care for now, she demonstrated the procedure. She placed the square on a table. A small, maneuverable table was in each examining room. The sterile linen-wrapped square was taped at one side with adhesive.

"You break this adhesive with your finger, not touching anything else," she said.

Then she took forceps obtruding from a tall metal cylinder of Zephiran on another table, grasped the edge of the broken adhesive with the forceps, gave a flip and turned the square over. Then, still with the forceps, she threw back each side of the sterile linen, revealing a small square stainless steel pan. In the pan was a small glass container which she lifted from the pan and, still with forceps, placed this on the linen beside the pan.

She lifted the surgical instruments from the pan, one by one, placing them on the linen. She left a small rubber bulb syringe in the pan and poured antiseptic solution and sterile water into the pan. Then into the glass container she poured surgical tincture.

These were the things the doctor would need for suturing (sewing) lacerations. The assisting nurse would give the doctor a sterile paper container holding sterile gloves and whatever size suture thread and needle the doctor requested. These were kept above the sink counter.

As she demonstrated, Miss Scarbrough cautioned me about not contaminating the set-up once the seal was broken and the items were open for the doctor.

"Be careful. Don't brush against it accidentally with your clothes," she said. "And don't let your hands touch anything on it. If it gets contaminated, we have to get a fresh one."

She smiled at me and said, "But I'm not worried about you. You can do it, with just a little practice."

But you cannot imagine how absolutely full of fear of contaminating that little surgical island I was. Instant panic would set in on me at the thought, and yet, I had to conquer it. For a long time I would plead for someone to oversee me when I was requested to do a suture set-up, to be certain I was doing it properly and not contaminating it.

You have never in your life seen such ginger stepping

around at arm's length. It was as though I were executing some exaggerated ballet step. Sort of a Pink Lady *pas de deux* with the surgical table. Perhaps it was comical to those who were more knowledgeable, but I certainly took my role seriously.

In such little ways, I was permitted a view and some participation in the mysterious healing circle. Since I am a non-medical person, everything magnetized me with the pull of a television drama.

Most people have the same fascination, I've found. Yet there is so much fear and misinformation about health care, especially about treating wounds, burns and the like.

Once I heard two interns talking. One said, "Do you know what she had on that sore when she came in? Cobwebs! She's a diabetic and couldn't get the cut on her hand to heal, so she covered it with cobwebs. Now it's really infected."

His mention of cobwebs on a wound reminded me of a day in November 1962 when I had interviewed a silver-haired woman of 84 years, Dr. Sarah Conyers Murray. She told me that in 1909 she had been the first woman medical student to attend the University of Tennessee. From her I first heard of the old-wives' tale practice of placing spider webs on an open wound, a sometimes deadly act.

Her story had beguiled me. She was an exceptional young woman to announce in 1909 to the college, "I'm going to be a doctor. I've come to earn a degree."

The board of registrars at the university had declared, she told me, "You can't. No woman has ever enrolled in medical school here."

The determination of the former school marm, then only recently widowed, outmatched that of the school. Not only

45

did she enroll, she earned her medical degree and graduated with a higher grade-average than any man in the class.

She said that later she had endured a rugged fight against the superstitions of rural folks.

"There were people who placed an ax under the bed, thinking it would make childbirth easier. There actually were people who used a 'mad stone.' They attached it to the wound of a victim of a rabid dog bite. It was horribly difficult to get a person to take rabies shots."

In the Emergency Room of Mobile General Hospital I recalled these things she had told me. She was really a remarkable woman and her words stuck strongly with me.

"One thing which really annoyed me," she had said, "was to arrive after being called, and find that an open wound had been covered with a bunch of grabbed-up spiderwebs by someone trying to be helpful before I arrived.

"It stopped the bleeding, all right, but it started infection which hurt the patient and made it harder for me to help."

I wondered if such folk remedies still were a problem, so when I had the opportunity I talked to Miss Scarbrough about it.

"People will come to the hospital after using harmful remedies," said Miss Scarbrough. "They smear butter or oil on burns. This is a very bad thing to do. And sometimes they make people vomit after they have swallowed a caustic substance. Not everything harmful that is swallowed should be forced up by vomiting. Some things yes, but not caustic substances."

She went on, "And applying iodine to an open wound causes the tissues to burn and results in slow healing."

I could remember when I was a child, iodine was immediately swabbed on every wound.

Miss Scarbrough said, "There's another home remedy that is harmful. Some people apply fat meat to nail punctures or abcesses. They think it will draw out the poison. Not only does this *not* draw out the poison, but the infection often goes on for a week or two before they come to us for help. Then the patient is worse off because of the wrong treatment and the prolonged wait."

It is odd, I thought, that fear, superstition and misinformation still cloud our attitudes about injury and disease. We think we live in an enlightened age—but there sat the diabetic woman in the Emergency Room with a wound covered by cobwebs.

Cobwebs. An appropriate symbol for our old fears and dusty illusions, I thought. Maybe that is why I had come myself to this place—to remove the cobwebs.

FIVE

At the limits of our knowledge, skill and science we find God. I remember another morning, in my second week, or third week. The rooms were filled when I arrived at 8:30 A.M. I greeted Miss Scarbrough and others and began my rounds.

A man of enormous girth lay on the bed in Room Seven. A very long, wide-ribboned strip of paper fell from his bed and ran across the floor. It was connected to the electro-cardiogram (EKG) that was monitoring his heartbeats.

A little while after I got there, Miss Scarbrough said, "Mrs. Greer, will you go in the anteroom and sit with the lady who has a blue dress on. Her husband has had a heart attack and he may not make it. I don't want her to be alone while she's waiting."

I walked into the room, a cubicle which was sometimes used by police officers while waiting for prisoner patients.

A Black woman, in her late fifties, sat in huddled isolation in the small room.

I smiled and said, "Miss Scarbrough wanted me to sit with you so you wouldn't be alone."

"Is Sonny all right?" she asked quickly.

"I just got here and I don't know," I said.

She began talking as I sat down in a chair beside her. "Sonny wasn't feeling too good when I left for work this morning, but he told me to go on. It was his day for a check-up and he planned to come to the hospital. So I went on."

She stopped, but not for long. "He's already had two heart attacks. He was doing so good and feeling real well lately. They called me at work and told me he had had another attack after he had arrived at the hospital. If I just hadn't gone on to work maybe I could have helped him."

"You did what he asked you to do. That's what's important," I said. "And he was here where they could give him the greatest help. They are doing all they can for him."

She said, "I know they are. I used to work here a long time ago. Well, not here. In the old Mobile General."

The door opened. Miss Scarbrough entered. Her face was somber. The woman asked anxiously, "How's Sonny? How's my husband?"

Miss Scarbrough said gently, "Mary, he didn't make it. The heart attack was too much."

The words began their shock effect slowly on the woman next to me. Miss Scarbrough said, "Mary, I want to give you a shot. It will ease you for a little while."

Mary gave a quick sound of dawning comprehension. "No," she screamed. "He can't be dead. He can't be." She began to cry.

She took the sedative administered by her friend, the E. R. Supervisor. Miss Scarbrough straightened up to leave the room. She looked at me and said, "Mrs. Greer, please stay with her awhile."

My arm went around the shoulders of the woman. As she moaned and wept disconsolately, my own eyes filled. She rocked back and forth, crooning, "Oh, Sonny. Oh, Sonny. If I hadn't left you this morning maybe you'd still be here. Oh, Sonny."

Her grief so engulfed me that I could not do anything but sit there, my arm about her shoulders, my hand patting her.

I thought, what is the matter with me? I can't seem to say any words of comfort, of hope. All I seem able to do is sit here and weep.

The door opened then. The maid on duty in the Emergency Room stood there. She was about my age. And such a lovely warm-hearted person. Each day when I came on duty she greeted me with the most beautiful smile and word of cheer. She would say, "Mrs. Greer, you're looking so pretty today." She would always make me *feel* pretty, when my mirror belied her words. And she always made me feel instantly welcome.

Now she gazed at the woman sitting there, a woman of her own race, her friend.

"Mary," she said in a tender, yet firm voice. "You got to get hold of yourself. We all have trouble sometimes, but we have to trust God. And call on Jesus."

"You call on Jesus to help you, Mary. He'll hear you. Jesus' always on time. He ain't never late. He's always on time."

The words were taking their effect on the woman beside

50

me. With my arm about her, I could feel the bodily-reaction of the still weeping woman. I could feel a slight lessening in the intensity of her rebellion against the grievous reality she was having to accept.

And I myself was filled with the impact of the words spoken so quietly, so fervently by this simple maid. It equaled that which I felt on leaving a worship service.

I felt so remiss that I had been unable to say the words to offer comfort to the weeping woman. In my heart I had felt them so strongly. But the words would not come, only the tears slipping down my face.

At the limits of our science there is faith. And Jesus.

After the woman left the anteroom, someone called and asked me to assist in Room Nine.

That's the reality of the Emergency Room. There is no time for prolonged grief or self pity—because you are called back to service.

A seven-year-old girl was lying on the stretcher. Her knee had been gashed in a bicycle accident. I was to help the mother hold the child steady, after the local injection of Xylocaine had deadened the wound for suturing.

The mother and I held the child's arms and shoulders firmly, and on my side of the stretcher-bed I steadied the girl's other leg. The doctor was suturing. The nurse was assisting. She clipped sutures as the doctor tied a small knot in every stitch.

The little girl could see the doctor's hand going up in the air with thread and instrument. I saw her eyes growing wide with fear.

She asked tearfully, "Is he taking it out?"

I realized what she meant. The doctor and the nurse

were intent on the operation at hand. They might not have heard the fear in the child's voice. I asked quietly and deliberately:

"Is he taking *what* out, Sweetie?"

"My *knee*," she said, faint with dread.

"No, the doctor is not taking your knee out," I said. The nurse and I grinned at each other. "He's fixing your knee all up and he's going to give you a pretty bandage to wear back to school. You can show all your friends your big bandage."

I added, "And you have been such a good girl."

The mother, who had kept her eyes turned away from the procedure, unable to bear to watch, now smiled as the doctor looked at the little girl and said, "You sure have been a good girl. Just about the best girl whose leg I ever sewed up," he teased.

Before the child was released, I gave her a huggable doll from the volunteer toy box.

She was young and fortunate and would be barely scarred by this, one of life's little mishaps. Children are so precious and vulnerable.

Later that same day Miss Scarbrough called me again. "I want you to go to the Retiring Room with me. I've got to give a shot to a woman whose child is having surgery for a brain tumor. She's very disturbed."

The words registered. Brain tumor. Was it Sally? Was it the pale-faced dear little girl I had met my first day in the Emergency Room, who had asked me if I were the Play Lady?

We entered the Retiring Room. When the young mother, who was painfully thin, saw the hypodermic needle in the nurse's hand she cried out, "No, no, I won't. Don't let her give me that. No, please." It was not Sally's mother. Miss Scarbrough said, "It's only a mild shot."

The husband tried to talk his wife into taking the sedative so it would calm her down during the ordeal of waiting. Evidently it had been he who had requested something to calm his wife's nerves.

The woman's whimpering increased. She rose up and moved behind a chair as though to protect herself and cried, "No, no, I'm going to pray to God to let my baby get well and he will."

Her husband said softly, "God will hear your prayer just as well with the shot."

She refused the sedative. After we left the room, Miss Scarbrough said, "She is very upset. She has refused to give her permission to operate for a long time. The doctors are afraid it may be too late."

We returned to the Emergency Room, the Supervisor to her specific ministering, I to checking rooms again.

As I went past Room Ten, I saw a frail infant on the heavy stretcher bed. Its bone-thin little arms were stretched upward as though beseeching someone to take it and hold it close.

The orderly stood on one side of the stretcher. The nurse's aide stood on the other side. They were both staring down at the infant with its tiny arms upraised. Neither moved, just stood there looking down. I paused to see if I could be of help, and suddenly I exclaimed, "Oh, it's not crying. What's the matter with it?"

The orderly, a tall angular young man, who was always impressively attentive to his duties, said in a way that seemed to me to be extremely biting:

"They can't tell us what the matter is when they come in like this."

The baby's rigid pleading posture etched itself in my brain.

As I walked quickly away from the room the nurse's aide followed me. I said, "He didn't have to speak so harshly about a poor little dead baby."

It was the first time I had taken a critical attitude about anyone in the Emergency Room.

The aide said to me in a low voice, "Mrs. Greer, he didn't mean anything by it. He was trying to cover up his own feelings. These things get to him and he doesn't like to show it. You'll come to realize that things touch him and he tries to hide it."

She was right. I was learning my lessons.

One person looking at another person simply cannot judge the interior of a heart. That is left for the One who grasped the upstretched hands of the sleeping infant and cradles it forever in his arms.

SIX

For decades Mobile General had been a guardian of the poor and stricken. It had worn many titles, Mobile City Hospital, Mobile County Hospital, Mobile General Hospital.

A large portion of its patients came from poverty level homes. Several were to become my special friends.

When I think of Mr. Grant, for one, I always think of that sweet line of verse that leaps into my heart. "Gentle Jesus, meek and mild."

That was Mr. Grant. Meek and mild. Eighty-one years old and suffering from a gall bladder disease that had turned his skin yellow. His hair was snow white. The first time I met him he said to me,

"I wish I had my Bible."

"Sir, I'll get a Bible for you right now."

I hurried to the volunteer office. High in a cabinet was a

stack of Bibles supplied to us by ministers and various organizations. There was always a Bible ready for some-one's use. And it was the patient's to keep if he or she wished.

I took the Bible into the room and handed it to Mr. Grant. He said to me, ''Thank you.'' He held the Bible gently in his hands.

''I love this book,'' he said. ''It's all I have, besides my dogs, a little pension and social security.''

His shock of feathery white hair framed his yellow-skinned face. One noticed the pale yellow immediately.

He said, ''I've got hepatitis.''

His was obstructive, not contagious, hepatitis. An in-tern told me later that Mr. Grant had come into the hospital after suffering from gall stones which had stopped the flow of bile from his liver for over two weeks.

He was a tall man, with a stalwart quality of strength in his face. His voice was feeble, but there was an essence of independence in it as he spoke. He had a strong chin.

His brown eyes had a troubled look about them. He opened his Bible and started turning through its pages. He looked at me and said, ''You know, I don't have to wear glasses. I can read my Bible without them.''

But now Mr. Grant had closed his Bible, holding it close. He seemed to want to talk, so I took the time and stayed a little while.

He said, ''I've been trying mighty hard to make it on my own. My wife died nine years ago and we never had any children. I've been doing for myself. I eat my three meals a day in a hamburger stand. That's not very good for any-body with gall bladder trouble. But it's the best I can do.

''I've been a hard worker all my life. I was an orphan at

thirteen, and from then on I worked in saw mills, in lumber camps. Later I got into the contracting business. But I'm old now.

"I'm eighty-one and it's just me and my dogs and my little house. After my wife died, I did all my housekeeping and my own cooking. About three years ago, it just got too much, and I started eating hamburgers." He might have been down, but he was not out. He still possessed some intrinsic vitality.

He went on. "Sometimes my neighbors would bring me food. But I've been having to spend more and more time in bed, just didn't feel very good. I didn't *want* to come over here to this hospital. I don't want anybody's charity. But my neighbors finally brought me. I was too sick."

I said, "Mr. Grant, this is a wonderful place and the doctors and nurses can do so much for you."

His eyes brightened into shining brown buttons, and he said, "I know that, young lady. They've been mighty nice to me. But," and here he paused a moment, "they want to operate on me. I know it. And I don't want that. All I want to do is go home to my dogs. I got ten of them."

I patted his shoulder and said, "They'll be waiting. You let us help you first."

As I walked out of the room, he was opening his Bible in a manner that indicated he was on intimate terms with its word and knew exactly where he wanted to turn for his comfort from the Lord.

I had looked on his chart and noted his address. I knew the neighborhood. For some reason, the fortitude and personality of this gentleman made me want to drive past his place on my way home that day. It would be a revelation of his rugged independence.

My other special friend also needed the charitable help of the hospital. I found her lying on a stretcher bed that day in another one of the examining rooms.

She was fifty-nine years old, and so emaciated that she looked like a skeleton. She had been brought in hemorrhaging from a cancerous throat long before I arrived. The hemorrhaging had been stopped. Soon she would be admitted to another ward to await surgery. Her eyes seemed to be searching deep into mine as I stood beside her for a moment.

Her voice, hoarse, raw, scratched its way into sound.

"Will you come to see me?" she asked.

The request startled me. I said, "Of course I will, my dear. This afternoon I will come up to your room." She closed her eyes.

I'll call her Catherine Collier (a fictitious name, as are many of the patients' names in this story, but she is a very real person).

Every time I think of someone's objection to the idea of a charity hospital, I think of these two remarkable people. How without the hospital they would have had nothing.

Later in the day, when things had slackened off a bit, I had time to see Catherine. She had been moved upstairs. I told Miss Scarbrough about our short conversation and asked if I could take a few minutes and go visit her.

Miss Scarbrough said, "Yes, you know we have a back-up volunteer coming in, in just a little while. You go on up to visit Miss Collier. She needs someone. She is really bad off."

Catherine Collier wanted to talk despite the throat cancer that made it so difficult for her. She seemed compelled to talk, so glad to see me, as though the very act of talking would draw human warmth and contact. There was no one else in the other beds at the time. How lonely this woman was. She looked like someone who was starving to death. For love, for food. I found that she almost was.

She was so gaunt it made me ache merely to look at her. But I tried to forget my own feelings, to become a responsive person for her. Increasing concern and sympathy tore at me as she talked.

"I've been begging potatoes from my neighbors to boil. My throat is so bad I could eat only soft foods. I have no money, no income, getting worse each day."

She spoke in whispers, and even then her voice was thin and very hoarse. She constantly used tissues to remove the phlegm from her mouth. Having to use tissues to remove matter from her throat and mouth in the presence of another person seemed to embarrass her terribly. She was a woman of genteel upbringing, from an affluent and prominent background of another southern city.

I was astounded. I could not believe it. Yet, she was here, the living, nearly dying, proof of life's hardships and inequities. She sat feebly upright on the side of her bed, beside the open drawer which held her little belongings, nose inhaler, throat salve, white mints.

This woman had a law degree. She had taught journalism in a college. She had a degree in English and Psychology. She had attended the School of Journalism at Columbia University and had been a free-lance writer for twenty years.

How could she have come from that wealthy, impressive background to this point—begging potatoes from neighbors, and starving to death—in America?

I sat there, incredulous as I listened to this lovely human

being trying so desperately to tell me her story. And to make sense of it for herself. Whenever I have been impatient with someone's pouring out his or her little life details, I've reminded myself of Catherine Collier. We all need people so desperately.

She said, "I waited two years too long to get help because I didn't have a dime, and I was too proud to ask for help, to ask for welfare. My parents were wealthy, my mother a lovely artist, my father a lawyer. I was an only child. I had everything." Now her arms and legs were so pitifully thin. One arm was connected, by tube, to the steady drip of sustaining glucose.

I wanted to stop her, to implore her not to talk, it was too hard on her. But something inside me knew that she wanted to talk to me. That she *must* talk to me, *to anybody*. She was an Ancient Mariner, with a tale she was compelled to tell.

She told me of her short-lived first marriage to a man who, as herself, was a free-lance writer. After this marriage ended, she continued her free-lance writing from the 1930's to the 1950's.

She later remarried and lived for five years in Europe. She became ill with tuberculosis in 1955 and returned to the United States. For five years she remained in a sanatorium. And her husband abandoned her.

She had received treatment and was dismissed, cured of the disease. In the meantime, her parents had died and left her a large sum of money. This, she said, had been in a joint bank account with her husband.

"He cleaned me out. I had no money left," she told me.

But with her creative resources at work during her

sanatorium stay, she had done a great deal of hand embroidery work, and she sold it.

"I saved a little money and came to Mobile," she said. She had lived for a time in Mobile when she was younger. She told me of frantic efforts and desperate ways she had tried to work, to eke out a little income after coming to our city.

But physically she was not able to work. She tried. Her small nest egg from embroidery work sales soon was swallowed by the expenses of living.

"I sold apples to school children for a few cents apiece," she whispered. The apples came from a friend she met at the farmer's market.

"Anything that was honest, I was willing to do." She added, "I'd even had a practical nurse's training. If I'd had a telephone I could have been in the registry."

Her voice wavered. "But I wasn't able to work."

She had to give up her apartment. Friends and acquaintances helped as much as they could, they took her in. Her condition and situation worsened. She had had a bad cold and sore throat. She was gargling with salt water, thinking she merely had a virus.

Four months earlier she had been rushed to Mobile General Hospital, hemorrhaging. She said, "They found I had an abcess, tumor and cancer in the tonsil and throat area around and below the ear."

Later she was released and then treated as an outpatient. She had applied for welfare. Meanwhile she lived with friends. For forty days she had received X-ray therapy for her cancer.

Catherine Collier looked at me, her thin face lined and

etched with pain, her mouth drawn and quivering. She begged, "Come back to see me. I've got to have surgery. Oh, please come back."

I felt an acute kinship. We were two women, two writers. But it was a cry of one human to another human as she added in a low whisper,

"Pray for me . . . your prayers . . ."

I touched her hand, held mine against hers for a moment, nodded mutely and turned to leave. My eyes were seeing through a blur of warm unbidden tears.

Slowly I walked down the hallway, Catherine Collier heavy in my mind and on my heart.

I looked at my watch. I had talked with her much longer than I had expected. My footsteps hastened toward the elevator, and I hurried back into the Emergency Room.

I paused for a while that afternoon in Ann Bennett's office. I was checking out and signing my hours for the day in the huge hours book. She smiled at me, her gorgeous infectious smile.

"Stay for a minute and let's chat," she said.

As I sat, or sagged, wearily in the chair beside her desk, she said, "At the rate you are going, spending six hours a day over here, it won't take you long to earn your hundred hours pin."

I hadn't heard of the pin before.

She said, "It's worn right above the embroidered insignia of hospital volunteers. Did you know that hospital auxiliary members all over the nation wear this emblem on their pink uniform or smock, beside their name tag?"

I did not. And then we fell into conversation in general about Pink Ladies. The whys and whereofs.

She said, "One of our volunteers earned a hundred

hours pin in a fantastically short time. She was a woman whose husband had just died, and she spent her time in hospital service to work out her sorrow.''

I learned there are many reasons that women all across America become Pink Lady hospital volunteers. A woman may have time on her hands with children in school. She may seek meaning outside housework. Her children may be grown and gone, as in my case. She may be alone, widowed.

Whatever the reason, she reaches out to the hospital with an offer to serve. And the hospital embraces her in its need. Ann told me that in the previous year alone, the donated services of volunteer Pink Ladies had saved Mobile General thousands of dollars in personnel expenditures.

"Ann," I said, "I am going home past the little place where Mr. Grant lives. I guess it's curiosity. He was in the Emergency Room today. You remember I got the Bible for him from the supply cabinet?"

She said, "Oh, yes. I remember Mr. Grant. Did you know that we found out through Social Services that the water pipes in his house froze and burst last March, and he's been without running water all this time. His neighbors have helped him."

I shook my head. "All he wants is to go back home to his dogs. He said he has ten dogs. Imagine! Ten dogs."

Ann said, "He really is awfully sick. They are trying to arrange through Social Services to get him a place in a nursing home so he will have proper care."

Later as I drove past the address where Mr. Imsand M. Grant lived, I slowed to a stop. What I saw was the house of a lonely man.

A ramshackle small lean-to house set at the back of a tree-covered lot grown high with weeds. A house where Mr. Grant had had no running water since last winter. A house where he lived and drew comfort from his Bible. And there in the yard were his dogs, short haired dogs, shaggy dogs, big, small; I could not count them all.

Some of them actually seemed to be climbing the chicken-wire fence that bound the small yard—waiting for their master's return, their master who loved them so. They were guarding his home until he returned to them.

Nailed to the sagging wooden gate was a sign of white cardboard with this lettered message: "Have Gone to Hospital. Check Across Street for any Business. I. M. Grant."

As I pulled slowly away from the curb where I had halted, I wondered, "Will dear Mr. Grant ever be able to come home to his beloved dogs?" I hoped so. I made a mental note to bring dog food the next day.

As I prepared supper for John and me that evening, all these people and their tribulations were on my mind. My mind could not be flipped like a switch. Turn off. Turn on.

John and I have a life-long habit of sharing everything. But I did not want to impose the troubles of so many others on my dear husband. And a Pink Lady should be discreet about the private affairs of hospital patients. She might discuss situations with the nurses, with the director of volunteers, but in all integrity, she should not discuss patients' personal business outside the hospital.

The ill and the dying deserve their privacy. Rich or poor their affairs should not be invaded. Even a charity patient. Especially charity patients who have to answer to so many impersonal bureaus and agencies. That is the reason for the changes of condition and names in this story. So I never spoke to John directly about anyone or used names. But that left me with many burdens.

My sleep was fitful and troubled that night as it was many nights after a hard day at the hospital. People floated across my dreams and dwelt within my unspoken prayers. I heard Catherine Collier's hoarsely whispered plea . . . "Pray for me."

And Mr. Grant's lament, "I wish I had my Bible."

I would wake and fall fitfully back into an exhausted half-sleep. I was constantly on the verge of tears. Yet I knew that my weary, finite love was of no tangible use to them.

I prayed, "Oh, God. You are strong and never weary and able to love and comfort all who cry unto you . . . even those with no voice with which to cry. Watch over us and keep us all the days of our lives and all the days of eternity."

SEVEN

The bulletin signboard outside the church I passed on my route to Mobile General Hospital every day always carried an axiom, epigram or encouragement. One morning as I passed the church, the words on the signboard were:

> BE KIND. EVERYONE YOU MEET IS
> FIGHTING SOME KIND OF BATTLE.

I would have reason to remember those words that day.

That day the Pink Ladies were to start a new branch of service. One of us was to sit at a hostess desk and assist families who were waiting out those long hours of concern for loved ones in Surgery, the Recovery Room, or the Intensive Care Unit.

I was asked to serve as the first Pink Lady in this new service. I would find that four hours at the hostess desk of Intensive Care and Surgery would drain me emotionally as quickly as seven hours in the Emergency Room.

The Pink Lady hostess had an OR (operating room) schedule of the patients who would be in surgery, the time and the type of surgery. She would make periodic reports to the waiting family members (via the Operating Room nurses at the Operating Room desk on the inside of the surgery complex). A typical report might be, "The surgery is about half completed, and should be finished in about 30 minutes."

Visitors were not permitted in the Recovery Room, but the Pink Lady hostess could check with the Recovery Room head nurse and relay comforting information to the family. And at the appointed brief times for visiting in the Intensive Care Unit, the hostess issued pink passes to the waiting family.

I always tried to familiarize myself with the people in the waiting room, careful to keep track of who was waiting for whom. Surgery, of course, is serious business, and so the concern of relatives is a very emotional situation.

I was especially alert on this new job because Ann Bennett had asked me to write my first story in the monthly newsletter, *The Pulse*, about the new hostess desk.

Winnie Smith, a friend of mine, was hospital Communications Director at that time. She put together and edited *The Pulse*. When my article appeared she used a small half-column photograph of me with the story I wrote.

While I was on duty that morning, I glanced up from my papers and saw a young girl being pushed past the desk in a wheelchair. I did not recognize the woman pushing the chair. It was not a volunteer, or hospital employee. But the young girl's head was blonde with very short hair. In the split second before she was moved beyond my range, I thought I recognized her. Then she was gone.

Was it Sally? So many people had crossed my life path in those days since I first met her. Perhaps I only thought I recognized her. I decided to check.

When Intensive Care visiting hours were over in mid-morning and morning surgery completed, I reported for duty in the Emergency Room.

In Room Nine a heavy teenager looked like a young ox on the stretcher when I first saw him. The nurse was pumping out the contents of his stomach. The notation on his chart read, ''pill ingestion.'' This could mean a suicide attempt, or of course, it could be accidental.

The Emergency Room was full and overflowing, and the nurse would be needed elsewhere. She asked, ''Mrs. Greer, would you do this?''

But this was an instance, a rare one, in which I resisted doing a task requested of me. She meant, would I take over the operation of the hand instrument by which she was drawing forth the poison from his stomach.

I could see what she was doing as she drew the huge suction syringe up, depositing the contents in a nearby basin. I could have done it. Yet something inside me rebelled. It was not mere physical repulsion, but the thought that I might do something, accidentally and unin-tentionally, to harm the boy.

I felt so embarrassed to say the words, ''I'm sorry, I just can't do that.''

She said softly, ''You can do it, Mrs. Greer.''

''I wish I could. Maybe I could, and I really hate to refuse, but I just can't do it.''

She saw my extreme discomfiture in refusing. She did not pursue it, but smiled reassuringly at me.

To remove all the poisoning element at that point, it was

necessary to remove everything. It took a long time for the suction to completely empty the stomach clean. Finally the youth was past any danger of overdose.

And as always when the twelve rooms were full in the Emergency Room, my help was needed in diverse ways.

Within a short while, the youth's stomach washing was completed and more seriously ill patients were waiting for rooms. He was wheeled on a light stretcher to one of the two long corridors fronting the examining rooms, to await his discharge.

I was flyaway busy as usual. But I became conscious of him as I passed by his cart from first one errand to another. I began to feel his eyes following me.

He was sprawled limply on the light cart. A restraining fabric strap buckled across his thighs prevented his falling off the stretcher.

He did not fight the restraints, but lay there, his head turning from side to side desultorily. His eyes magnetized on me as I moved in and out of his vision.

"Lady, are they going to take me to the mental unit?"

"Son, I don't know. I am a volunteer and I am just helping."

"Lady, please don't let them take me. If they take me to the Holcombe Unit, they'll send me to Bryce. And lady, I just can't go back to Bryce. I promise I won't ever do this again. I promise, lady."

The Holcombe Mental Unit at that time was the Mobile General Hospital holding unit for mental patients. Bryce Hospital is an Alabama state mental hospital located at Tuscaloosa.

(The Seventh Floor Psychiatric Center of Mobile General Hospital was, as I mentioned, not completed at that time. Later it would be operated through a cooperative program of the Mobile Mental Health Center, Dr. William H. Simpson, Administrator; and Mobile General Hospital.)

The young fellow kept saying, "Lady, you don't know what it's like to be sent away. I've been there. I can't stand it if I have to go back. Lady, I promise I won't ever do it again."

Then he said, "Ma'am, can I see my mother? Can my mother come back here with me?"

I told him I would find out. When I asked Miss Scarbrough, she said, "Let me check with the doctor first, Mrs. Greer."

She did, and then told me that the doctor said, "He can't see anyone now."

She added, "This patient has been treated here before and the doctor thinks it best that he not see anyone now, not even his mother."

When Miss Scarbrough said that, for some strange reason some words came suddenly into my mind. Words spoken by a psychiatrist I had interviewed for a series of newspaper stories on mental health. The words had haunted me ever since Dr. Claude Brown had spoken them.

He said, "Home is where the heart is, but it is also where the *heat is on*. Families generate the things that grind people to pieces."

Home is where the heat is on.

Family members get caught up in life struggles and daily pressures and demands, and in the process, grievous psychological wounds can be inflicted.

Parents suffer. Children suffer. All within the framework of the home. Where the heart is. Where the heat is on.

One person out of every ten in America is, or will be a patient in a mental institution at some time. One half of all the hospital beds in our country are taken up by the mentally ill.

It follows that some of the acutely distressed persons will show up in the Emergency Room of a general hospital. Their behavior may suddenly become unacceptable, or withdrawn, or violent. They demand attention, and the hurts that have festered can no longer be ignored.

In many instances, family members and relatives will be oblivious of warning signals, or they may believe that by ignoring them everything will work out, and the disturbing behavior will go away.

Mental illness is not restricted to any one age group or economic level. It goes the gamut, from autistic little children, to overly rebellious teenagers, to frustrated frantic young adults, to bewildered, confused middle-aged people, to the muddled and senile.

It is America's number one health problem and was called the ''great unfinished business'' in a five-year-study by Congress on the national mental health picture as revealed in its *Joint Commission on Mental Illness Report* of 1961. One might say that it is still an unfinished business.

The youth in the Emergency Room now, was one of these who so desperately needed help.

He implored, ''Please, ma'am, don't let them take me to

Bryce. I swear I won't ever do that again. I swear it."

I said, "You listen to the doctors and nurses. Maybe you won't have to go back."

I smiled at him as I moved away. Each time I passed by him I would smile briefly and nod my head to him.

He was an "HMU Consult." This meant that the Intern on duty in the Emergency Room wanted a consultation with the Resident on duty in psychiatry connected with the Holcombe Mental Unit.

Tragedy comes every day to Emergency Rooms from the lives of men and women, young and old, who find themselves in emotional dead-ends. Suicide attempts, alcoholism, the paranoid, schizophrenic.

Mental health professionals say that generally there are two or possibly three common ways in which people come to the brink of despair, through mental strain. It can be cumulative, building up over a long period of time. It can be brought on in a sudden catastrophe which serves as a trigger. And many doctors believe it can be caused by an improperly balanced body chemistry.

I remember vividly a pretty woman, about thirty years of age. I saw her for only a few moments, as she was standing at the Emergency Room admitting desk. She was diminutive in size, with pale brown hair. As she stood there smiling elatedly, her dark-haired husband stood beside her, giving information to the woman behind the desk. His face showed strain.

The young woman was telling all within hearing distance of "my wonderful box I've invented."

She said, "I can go back into any period of time I want

72

to. I went back to the time that little baby Jesus was born. I saw Mary. I actually saw Mary. She was holding the little baby and smiling. I saw her myself.''

The young woman apparently was in happy agitation. She beamed. She smiled. As I walked away on my errands, I heard her say, ''My husband wants me to tell the doctor about my wonderful box.''

Her husband was obviously concerned and had brought her to the Emergency Room for consultation.

What strange chemistry, or catastrophe, or cumulative erosion of self had brought the young woman to try to escape this world through her transporting box? All of us transport ourselves away from tension in some fashion. For some the TV box is our transporting box. Or alcohol. Or drugs. But this woman's behavior was beyond the acceptable norm. And help had to be sought.

On another morning, in the middle of my routine work, Miss Scarbrough had said, ''Mrs. Greer, will you go in Room Six and stay with that lady? Her husband needs to use the phone and I don't want her left alone.''

As I entered the room, pushing the heavy door open, the husband, a tall graying man, smiled wanly, started to leave and said, ''I'll be right back, just as soon as I can.''

He wasn't looking at me as he spoke; his eyes were turned in tormented solicitude to his wife lying on the stretcher bed. She reposed with her head and shoulders leaning upright against the raised back, as though she were on a chaise lounge.

She gave him no recognition. She shut her eyes tightly, as though denying his existence. He stared at her a mo-

73

ment. He seemed on the edge. Then he left the room.

The woman appeared to be about sixty years old. She was short and her hair was gray. She was wearing a bright yellow nylon quilted robe, yellow nylon pajamas showed beneath. Matching yellow slippers were on her feet. No sheet covered her still body. Her hands rested, clasped, across her breast.

She looked for the world like a sweet obedient little girl lying there, except for her face, touched indelibly with criss-cross age lines. Her closed eyes were red rimmed.

But at the moment she was not crying. I said, "That is such a pretty robe you have on. I just love it."

She opened her eyes, looked at me. Then quickly she closed them again. It was as if she were shutting me and the world out.

I moved over to the sink counter quietly in my rubber-soled shoes and glanced at the counter and shelf supplies. Habit made me scan an area for needed supplies. As I did, I noted the capitalized letters at the top of the patient's chart resting on the counter.

The letters were "HMU Consult."

Then suddenly the room was filled with the rapid staccato of words rushing from her lips very quietly.

"Walk softly with mother. Dear God, You know I am not a praying woman since I was a child at my mother's knee and she said to me, 'Child, say your prayers and fold your hands and talk to God. Tell Him all your problems and He will help you and I'll stay right here until you tell God all about it . . .' A lot of people think I'm not a

Christian because I don't go to church and take part in lot of things, but You know I'm a Christian, God.''

Then abrupt silence.

Her eyes were shut tight. Her lips were working silently. They formed mute words that apparently she was hearing in her mind.

Then all at once the words burst forth again.

''But you've told me, God, that I must fight and I'm not giving up. I'm holding on, God, you've told me to keep fighting.''

All the time, as rapid-fire as a machine gun, the words spewed out, stumbling over themselves in agitation. I stood motionless lest I startle her with my presence and interrupt her prayer.

In a little while the consulting doctor entered. I remained in the room. He spoke to the distressed woman.

''Mrs. East, do you know where you are?''

She opened her eyes. Without moving her head, she let her eyes roam the room in their orbit.

''It—it—it's the chapel of Calvary Cross Church. Yes, it's Calvary Cross Church chapel.''

''Now,'' said the doctor gently, ''does this look like a church chapel to you? Does it really look like a chapel? Look around you.''

(Actually, the examining rooms were the starkest rooms imaginable, designed to meet medical emergencies, not create esthetic views.)

This time the woman turned her head and stared all about the room and said hesitantly, ''No, I guess it looks like a hospital. I guess that's where I am.''

"That's right," said the doctor. "Do you know your name, who you are?"

"My name is Evelyn East."

The doctor said, "What day is it, Mrs. East? Do you know the date and the day of the week?"

Immediately she spit out the words, "It's Tuesday, the fourteenth. I know what day it is. It's Tuesday, the fourteenth."

The woman's husband walked into the room as she spoke these words. He said quietly to the doctor, "Her mother died on Tuesday the fourteenth. But that was six weeks ago. She got this way after her mother's funeral in Calvary Cross Church."

Then, the words that the dear beset woman had poured forth when I was alone in the room with her made sense to me. Evidently her mother's death had been a shock to her and she was sorely troubled. It may have been odd, but she was working it out in a form of prayer.

When her husband had returned, I left for other duties. I did not see the woman any more that day. But a day or so later, as I was wheeling a patient upstairs, I saw her sitting in the interior X-ray corridor, apparently waiting for tests.

I smiled at the woman and she broke into a smile of greeting and threw her arm up and waved at me.

Suddenly a warmth filled me and I felt in tune with the world. I had the express feeling that the woman was getting help and that she would be all right.

I could identify with her. I felt loss too—my daughter's leaving home. Changes in our lives often create stress that is temporarily unbearable. Some days in Intensive Care or the Emergency Room left me on the verge.

At any age particular problems occur. The struggles for self-hood in some of our youth today seem so rugged and rebellious. I did not know that obese young man's circumstances. But I saw in him youth's frightening gropings for personhood and dignity. I happened to be there when the boy was dismissed.

Miss Scarbrough said, "Mrs. Greer, will you unbuckle the strap on the boy and help him out front to his mother. He's ready to go."

I went to the stretcher in the back corridor, and unbuckled the fabric strap and assisted him off the stretcher. He lumbered along beside me. I guided him by the arm.

In the outside lobby he brightened as his mother approached him. Her face was a blank. You could read nothing in it. She said, "I need a cigarette."

He said, "Mama, give me some money and I'll get some for you from a machine."

"Never mind," she said, "I've got to check you out at this desk here."

I stepped back, relinquishing him to his mother. I smiled at them both. "Where the heat is on," I thought. I wondered what this sad, overweight, self-destructive young man was tormented by.

I turned to go back into the Emergency Room. As I pushed open the door I was remembering the statistic. One person out of every ten is, or will have to cope with mental illness. And I remembered the sign I had seen earlier that morning:

"Be Kind. Everyone you meet is fighting some kind of Battle."

EIGHT

When I walked into Ann's office later that afternoon, she was sorting through a huge box in one corner of the room. It was filled with stuffed animals in a riot of yellows, reds, blues, greens; giraffes, elephants, dogs, cats, bears tumbled out or dangled and peered over the sides of the box, ready for some child's hands to reach eagerly for them.

Ann looked up at me and grinned.

"Believe it or not, even though it's July, some of this is for Christmas. The people in this town are so generous. Club men and women do so much for the patients. And some of them start supplying us for Christmas as early as the summer. They are just great!"

Later we went to the cafeteria, seated ourselves at a corner table and talked over coffee. Ann began telling me about Christmas time in Mobile General.

"The entire hospital takes on a happy look," she said. "Christmas decorations appear overnight. Every department in the hospital is decorated by the Pink Ladies."

She talked animatedly. Her vivacity and joyful pride in the hard work of the volunteers showed.

I could see the hospital through her eyes—departments one by one suddenly glistened and shone with Christmas. Lab, clinics, Emergency Room, that magnificent lobby and curving stairway festooned with greenery, and huge Christmas decorations all put on a festive face. Expectant children's voices filled the air as volunteers prepared gifts.

She said, "The closer it gets to Christmas, the more clubs there are throughout the city who send in their annual contributions of gifts for patients of all ages, not just the children.

"And the Emergency Room party. You'll love the Christmas party. The entire Emergency Room staff exchanges presents. The Emergency Room volunteers have their gift exchange. And the food. You wouldn't believe it.

"Miss Scarbrough is the most wonderful cook and people from other departments come into the party—it's held in the doctors' dining room—just to get a taste of some of her cooking. All the Emergency Room nurses and some volunteers bring covered dishes. The Emergency Room party at Christmas is really something to look forward to."

Ann laughed again. "Even in July," she added.

I remembered that Ann had said when she guided the church teenagers on that tour, "I usually begin a tour with the Emergency Room, for it is the heart of the hospital."

79

I was coming to see for myself that it did personify the "heart" of the hospital. The instant source of aid to those who came asking for help. And a merry heart, apparently, as well. At least at Christmas.

I was beginning to see in a new light the way people who suffer and those who serve in the midst of suffering always strive toward life, toward joy, toward creating a more human, more caring community.

Later as Ann and I walked from the cafeteria to her office, I remembered Catherine Collier and Mr. Grant. I asked her about them.

Ann said, "Catherine Collier is going to have surgery on Monday, I think. And Social Services has found a nursing home for Mr. Grant. He was released from the hospital yesterday."

She added, "But he'll probably be back for surgery if he will ever consent. The doctors want to operate. But so far he's refusing. Just talks about wanting to get back home to his dogs."

"Bless them both; I hope they make it," I prayed.

"Ann," I asked. "Do you remember a little blonde girl, about eleven? She had a brain tumor."

"Yes," she said. "Sally's here. You'll have to see her."

I would.

After coffee I made a couple of deliveries to the lab, and on my way back to the Emergency Room I slipped in for just a moment into the small chapel located on the first floor.

I sat down on a rear pew. I was thinking of Catherine Collier and her surgery on Monday morning. I would be on duty on the first shift as Operating Room-Intensive Care Unit hostess.

In the dimly lit chapel I began to think of how much the chapel itself must mean to so many people. And as I looked about me, I thought of how the chapel came to be.

There had been no chapel at Mobile General Hospital when the new building was constructed. But when Dr. Billy Hightower arrived as Mobile General Hospital's first head of Cardiovascular Surgery to institute and direct open heart surgery, he asked for a chapel.

There was no money for one. But where there is a heart (and a will) there is a way. Dr. Hightower had told his wife of his concern for a chapel. She conferred with Director of Volunteers, Ann Bennett, and the Rev. Francis B. Wakefield, Episcopalian minister and Chairman of the Chaplaincy Advisory Council.

Mrs. Bennett promptly vacated a small supply room on the first floor to house the chapel.

Mrs. Hightower was referred by someone to Mr. V. W. McGwier of Grove Hill, Alabama, some 85 miles from Mobile, a maker of church furniture. Mr. McGwier came to Mobile, measured the chapel room, made sketches.

"We have no money," said Mrs. Hightower.

Like a Carpenter of Nazareth, the furniture craftsman had said, "It is my privilege to do this for Mobile General."

He custom made and donated the beautiful mahogany-finished pews, lectern, altar and altar rails.

Someone else gave a carpet of deep aqua. Soft lighting accents appeared. Pink Ladies contributed a cross, candles, a picture of Christ. One gave a beautiful Bible in memory of her husband.

The chapel was ready, open for people in quiet and desperate circumstances who turned to God in the silence of the room.

I sat there a few moments with Catherine Collier deep in my heart, remembering her rasping and hoarsely spoken words. I prayed.

"Oh, Dear Heavenly Father, be with her. Help her. Sustain her with your love. Your love so great you gave your Son, who knew suffering for each of us. Touch her with thy presence, dear Father. Amen."

I eased out of the pew and hurried back to the Emergency Room. Then as I walked down the hallway, I saw Sally's mother.

Her face brightened into a smile as she saw me. We stopped.

"Hello there," I said.

"Mrs. Greer," she said. "I found out your name. I read the little article in the hospital newspaper this morning and saw your picture. I knew it was you.

"Sally told me she saw you when she went to X-ray this morning. She's upstairs now in her room."

I said, "I *thought* that was Sally, but I didn't recognize the woman pushing the wheelchair, so I wasn't sure. How is she?"

"She's not doing well."

"Oh, I am so sorry."

"The X-rays may tell us something. And I think they're going to do a myelogram, too, to get the whole picture. The lady who was with Sally is a friend from Oklahoma. She's almost like family, like a sister."

I said, "Is there anything I can do, is there anything I can get for Sally?"

"Well, she has been wishing for some Old Maid Cards."

"I'll get some for her before I leave here," I said.

Sally's mother went on up to the room. I turned toward the auxiliary gift shop, purchased some Old Maid Cards, then headed upstairs in one of the front elevators.

When I pushed open the door and walked toward Sally's bed, she opened her arms wide. She threw them around my neck as I bent toward her, and hugged me in a time embrace.

"Mama, it's my Play Lady."

When she said those words, my eyes filled with tears. *Dumb tears*, I thought. *Why can't I seem to control myself?* My heart just seemed to turn inside out with her words. I put the Old Maid Cards in Sally's hands and stood there smiling. I looked at her through a blur.

"Sally, you're looking so pretty," I said. Then she had to tell me several stories. She did not seem at all frightened of the hospital as she had before. Then we played a game of Old Maid.

"I have to go now," I said, "but I'll see you next Monday."

I was happy to see her again, but sad that it was under these circumstances. She was the little girl I no longer had. A fragile blessing to her parents and to me.

I walked out of the hospital and drove home with her image and words ringing in my heart.

NINE

Children are so precious that their ills affect us more emotionally than our own. One of my greatest dreads was always to hear about accidents, about burns that happen so frequently to children even in the protective environment of the home.

Too often these accidents end in tragedy, but one story I had covered while a reporter and before I came to Mobile General as a volunteer still encouraged me about the wonders of medicine and faith to preserve and restore life.

I remember that little girl, Kathy. Her story contained all the ghastliness of what can happen to children through unintentional carelessness, and all the hope that can come from loving care.

First I saw the photo, a stark photograph of a little girl standing in her baby bed in the Burn Unit at the old Mobile General. The photograph was taken by a news photographer, with permission of the child's parents, through the glass wall of the unit. Sterile conditions would permit no outsiders within the unit itself.

The city editor had passed by my desk and paused when he saw the photo lying there on the edge of the desk. He stood, immobilized, his own face a reflection of pain as he looked, magnetized by the sight of the scarred body of the child as she stood in her baby bed, wearing only a diaper.

He said softly, ''That picture ought to be run on the front page of the paper.''

It had happened in a small town some fifty miles from Mobile. The 23-month-old blonde girl was on the back seat of the car, when her mother got out of the car and went into the filling station, that spring morning about 10:30 A.M.

With a toddler's natural curiosity, Kathy explored all the crevices of the back seat. She found some stray matches.

A few minutes later the little girl had ignited her dress and was turned into a flaming torch.

The screams of the toddler alerted her mother, who grabbed her, carried the burning child to the ground, and tried to smother the fire by rolling the screaming child in the dirt, while beating the flames with her hands.

Then aided by the gas station attendant, she put the child on the car seat and in frantic haste sped to the hospital in her small town. There, the doctors looked at the child and told the mother: ''She is so badly burned, we can't take care of her. You'd better take her to Mobile. Mobile General Hospital is equipped to take care of her. And she needs help fast.''

The ambulance was called, the child's father was located and they rushed to Mobile.

At Mobile General, the child was taken directly into the

examining room. Swift, gentle and skilled hands of attending physicians and nurses went to work on the little girl.

She had sustained first, second and third degree burns of the face, right arm, trunk and thighs.

Vital steps were taken to save her life. A tracheotomy was performed. This is almost always done when deep burns are on the face. It indicates that there may be damage to the windpipe which could prevent free breathing. A tube is inserted into the windpipe through the neck below the voice box.

Her blood pressure was taken. A blood count and type for cross-matching was taken for the lab. A cutdown into the vein started her on 500 cc's of blood. Glucose was begun also by I.V. (intravenously).

She was given antibiotics and lockjaw shots.

She was weighed. This is imperative to gauge weight loss through intravenous fluid-therapy which was to follow.

A urinary catheter was inserted. For the first few weeks every bit of fluid intake and output of the patient would be measured as part of the progress chart.

Because of little Kathy's restlessness, both from pain and from fear of strange surroundings, leg and arm restraints were used to protect her from hurting her damaged tissue and from pulling the endotracheal tube, glucose and other tubing from their places.

Doctors began the initial debridement next. This is an operation to remove the burned skin.

Next, Kathy was taken on a stretcher with sterile sheets to X-ray for a chest film. From there she was moved immediately to the Burn Unit. That would be her home for the next 83 days.

The Burn Unit is an antiseptic world. No one enters except medical personnel in sterile cap, gown, mask. They scrub up, wear gloves, and in the old hospital, stepped on a disinfectant rubber sponge made to cut down infection even from the soles of shoes, before entering.

All procedures in the Burn Unit are for sterile conditions. This is mandatory because death can result sometimes, not from the burn itself, but from infection of the highly sensitive burned areas. Every precaution is taken to prevent infection.

Kathy was put to bed in sterile linens, with a cradle over her to prevent the sheet touching her body. She was in a large baby bed with rungs on the sides.

In the Burn Unit, Kathy began vomiting. A doctor inserted a tube to a slow suction pump to keep her stomach empty. Here too the output was measured. Part of the exact charting in fluid-therapy. Kathy was to receive nothing by mouth.

Meanwhile in the corridor outside the Burn Unit, Kathy's parents were assured that everything possible was being done for their child by doctors and nurses especially trained to care for burned patients.

The doctors explained the seriousness of their child's condition, and the importance of their having no contact with her because of the possibility of infection. They were permitted to view their child through the observation window of the Burn Unit.

Inside the Burn Unit, which then in the old hospital

housed eight beds and much special equipment, Kathy was in serious condition.

She was receiving medical care, constant and tender loving care from doctors. Almost every kind of specialist was involved: reconstructive plastic surgeons, staff physicians, interns, residents and dedicated nurses.

And through it all, from the moment her dress flashed into flames, Kathy never lost consciousness. She had suffered everything totally awake, without even the relief of unconsciousness.

Routine lab cultures and sensitivity tests of the burned areas determined what drugs would be used in the battle for her life.

Burns of the face and respiratory tract are particularly dangerous burns. Some critical days were ahead for Kathy. Within two days, she was receiving more blood, I.V. fluids and special care for the tracheotomy tube.

As soon as is possible, the burned patient is allowed to eat by mouth. But Kathy, frightened by the strangeness of the place, refused to eat. She was fed through a tube. The nurses gently encouraged her to eat, and soon she was eating a bit in addition to the tube feeding.

Eleven days after she arrived at the hospital, Kathy was placed in a vibrating bath with medication in the water. The circulating water washes away the formation of the crust on the burns of the patients. This was done every twelve hours.

A week later, Kathy underwent surgery for debridement (removal of all excessive dead tissue—eschar—of a deep burn) of the body and face, chest and abdomen.

For the first time, dressings were applied to her burns. A

week later, dozens of postage-stamp-size skin grafts were applied.

Five days later, Kathy suddenly became seriously ill. Her temperature shot up to 105 degrees. This is not unusual in critical burns, but it is extremely dangerous.

All dressings were removed. She was back on tub baths. Her condition worsened. She became critically ill. Blood was transfused and the continuing constant watch was kept on her, as it is with all patients in the Burn Unit.

For five days she was extremely ill. Then, miraculously, she began to improve, rapidly.

Later there would be more surgery, skin grafts. She was eating again and talking her little girl talk. Then, she was able to sit up in bed; next she was bouncing around the sides of her baby bed.

She was a dear, sweet, smiling child. Still unaware that now her smile was twisted grotesquely by burns on one side into a grimace. She loved the nurses. And she was one of the darlings of the Burn Unit. She played happily with sterilized rubber toys. And with her parents and many praying for her, she began to heal.

Now she was able to look intensely about her at this strange place, her Burn Unit home. To observe seriously the no-longer strange figures with the caps on their heads, gloves on their hands, masks across their faces.

They had brought her back from near-death with tender skill, special equipment and by working around the clock.

Mothers of children who have been burned will talk almost with reverence in their voices regarding the loving devoted care of nurses in the Burn Unit.

Kathy looked at the others in the Burn Unit. A little girl

lay under a sterile sheet-covered cradle. She had been burned by sparklers, 45 percent of her body with third degree burns.

Other children were victims of hot grits pulled over on themselves, hot gravy, scalding hot coffee, trash fires, explosions, electrical burns. They were here together.

Then it was Kathy's birthday. Kathy's mother brought a cake. There were candles, two of them on it. But the candle tapers remained unlighted, untouched by the flicker of a match. What child could bear the traumatizing sight of candle flames in the Burn Unit? Surely not children who had known the terror of flames leaping at them.

The nurse cut the cake and Kathy's fun was shared with the other youngsters who were able to eat. Kathy's mother, eyes doubtless brimming with tears of prayerful thankfulness, watched the drapes-drawn-back window.

In the weeks that followed, Kathy steadily improved. Exactly 83 days after the fateful fire, Kathy went home with her mother and father.

Her little smile was still twisted. There would be more reconstructive surgery in the future for her. But she was a happy child, squealing in laughter, able to walk and run with exuberant childish joy because of the hospital's quick, professional response.

It is the stories of such wonderful healings and successes that kept me on the job as a volunteer.

TEN

Monday morning. This was the day that Catherine Collier and Sally were to face surgery. I arrived at the small waiting area for OR-ICU; there sat Sally's mother and the family friend.

Even before I plugged in the portable phone I held in my hand and put my papers in order, to get down to the hostess business at hand, I greeted Sally's mother, smiled at her friend, and inquired about Sally.

"How's our darling girl?" I said.

"She's in surgery," said her mother. "They are doing an exploratory to see if they can find the cause of the constant pain she has in her back."

I glanced down the surgery schedule I held in my hands. Sure enough, there was Sally's name, scheduled for laparotomy at 8 A.M.

There was no one else in the waiting room, a rarity outside Surgery and Intensive Care. But it was early, 8:30 A.M. The surgery schedule was light and Intensive Care visiting hours were not until ten.

The family friend and Sally's mother were discussing Sally. The friend said, "You let her get away with too much. You ought to discipline her more."

I remembered that I had heard one of the floor nurses commenting about the little girl who was screaming at her mother and scratching her. I saw the scratch on Sally's mother's arm. She said to her friend, "There'll be plenty of time to discipline her if it's necessary, later. I just don't think discipline is necessary now."

She looked at me. I nodded my head in agreement.

"I think you are right," I said. "The pain in some conditions can cause abnormal behavior; that may be why she is unruly. I think you are right to be patient with her."

Then no more was said on that subject. The waiting room began to fill, and I was busy obtaining information from those waiting. Then word from Surgery and Intensive Care personnel had to be relayed to the waiting families.

Sally had been taken from Surgery into Recovery before I left. I did not learn the result of the operation just then.

I told Sally's mother, "I'll check with you later on. I have to go on duty in the Emergency Room now. If there is *any* way I can be of help, please let me know. You can get me from the Emergency Room if you need me, or check with the volunteer office."

She said warmly, "Virginia, if I need you, I will surely

call you. It means so much to me, just knowing you are here."

I returned the portable phone and the surgery schedule to Ann Bennett's office, along with the pink passes to Intensive Care. The next OR-ICU hostess would pick them up. I was due now in the Emergency Room.

"Ann," I said, "Sally was operated on this morning."

"Yes, I know."

I thought, "What's the matter with me. Of course, she knows. She gets the surgery schedule before I do."

I said, "Maybe we can learn what they found. I'll check with you later. That little girl is very dear to me."

Something was on my mind. But I couldn't quite tell what it was. It was nagging at me.

As I walked hurriedly down the hallway to the Emergency Room, I kept trying to think what it was. There was something important. But I couldn't describe it. I pushed open the wide door of Emergency Room and then, as usual, was caught up in the flood waters.

Every July, a tidal wave of new interns surges into teaching hospitals all across the country. They have completed their medical education, pre-med, medical school, state board exams and have earned their degrees. But internship and residency still lie ahead for them, constituting more on-the-job training before they go into practice or research.

I always think of this when I hear someone say, "I don't want an Intern working on *me*." An intern is a medical doctor. He's earned his wings. And is furthering his knowledge in his field by daily ministering personally to the variety of diseases he had studied and dealt with in his years of medical school.

And in a teaching hospital, such as Mobile General, there are always those physicians of long time medical practice, in any specialized field, who can be called on at a moment's notice if needed for consultation.

One of the interns that summer had been a long time schoolmate of my son Jerry. They had been in Sunday school together through the years, and had ridden motorcycles together. Daring, full of courage and, as most parents fear, possibly foolhardy. They had both graduated from college, and this young man had gone on to medical school. He was now back, interning at Mobile General Hospital.

I always had to restrain my delight on seeing him at the hospital. He'd smile whenever he saw me and then greet me cordially. And I would hold back on calling him "Tom," and address him as "Doctor." Anyone who has earned the degree deserves to be called doctor.

One day he stopped by the table in the cafeteria as I was sitting at lunch with Miss Scarbrough.

"Mrs. Greer, I want you to meet my wife."

His bride was so beautiful, a graduate R.N., from another city. Of course, Miss Scarbrough already knew both of them. And it was all I could do to keep from standing up and hugging them both. Somehow from contact with this young man in his growing-up years, in the church and with my son, I felt a motherly feeling toward him. Now I felt that way about his wife.

Later he stopped by my table in the cafeteria and said,

"Mrs. Greer, tell Jerry I have been doing some scramble trail riding on the motorcycle. And tell him I said it's not for me."

"Where were you riding? And what kind of motor did you ride?" I asked.

"It was over at the Gulf, and I was riding a Yamaha. But tell Jerry it's not for me, not anymore."

"I'll tell him," I said. "Jerry has moved to California and is working in the motorcycle industry there. He's still racing motors on the weekends and writing articles about the races. He loves it out there."

That afternoon Dr. Tom was on duty in the Emergency Room, and at one point he asked me to get an ear speculum for him. I raced through a door into the examining room, and as I nearly collided with an orderly, I threw my hand behind me smack into the back-crack of the closing door. I saw stars, rockets and comets.

Gritting my teeth, tears springing from my eyes, I was whisked into a room, ushered onto a stretcher, given a shot of Xylocaine in the finger to deaden it. Here was one case of progress I regretted—I would have been better off with old green curtains they'd had at the old Mobile General.

The anesthetic was not necessary. The crunch had done its own deadening. Then came the suturing by an intern, four stitches on one side of the finger, three on the other. A bandage was added. I got down off the stretcher and went about my duties.

Miss Scarbrough was the one who saw to it that her fallen Pink Lady had received prompt medical aid. There was a singular affection between us, volunteers, nurses, interns in the Emergency Room and Miss Scarbrough.

If the Emergency Room was the heart of the hospital, Miss Scarbrough was the heart of the Emergency Room.

Interns were quick to learn about the remarkable sustaining qualities of this Christian woman and they learned to benefit from her experience.

The rapport between them was touching. She never encroached. She never intruded. She was there. And they knew it, to their increasing advantage.

This, obviously, was not turning out to be my day.

And then I heard about Catherine. She had died. This woman writer whose life had been of such unbelievable sequential distress, unhappiness, wretchedness, suffering, despair. I kept thinking of her. Of her incredible courage and pride in the face of alienation and insurmountable odds.

In my emotional state, I began to selfishly let myself almost go to pieces. I felt the grief welling up in me.

I couldn't face any more that day. I checked to see about Sally. She would remain in Intensive Care at least overnight. I decided to go home.

When I signed out, in the hours book in Ann Bennett's office, she was not there.

"I'll have coffee or lunch with her tomorrow," I thought, as I wrote in the hours I'd spent at work. "I'll apologize for walking out like this."

But I knew in my heart no apology was necessary.

Friends, especially among volunteers in a hospital never needed apologies. The grievous burdens of humanity were so prevalent, widespread, yet so pervadingly singular and individual, that every Pink Lady, every volunteer felt it and knew it. And understood.

And I was only *one* Pink Lady. Ann Bennett was in contact with all of them. All over the hospital.

Only now was I truly beginning to understand the personal torments and anguishes that Ann Bennett and Helen Scarbrough had to endure constantly, and yet somehow they continued to smile and go about their ministries.

I drove home weeping, driving with extreme care because of the emotional state I was in. I'd seen the tragic results of emotion-induced automobile accidents. I tried not to think about Sally, because I was dreading the worst.

When I went into the Emergency Room the next morning, I looked for Miss Scarbrough. Such a wonderful person, so filled with Christ's love. She would understand, even though I would not take a lot of time explaining.

"When I get caught up on checking the rooms and getting supplies into the needed places, and run whatever errands you need, I want to take a few minutes and go up and see Sally," I told her. "I promised her mother I'd check with her."

Miss Scarbrough said, "That will be fine. Just let me know when you go."

And so, later that morning I knocked softly on the door of the hospital room and Sally's mother came out.

"Oh, Virginia," she said. And we put our arms around each other, and stood there a moment. "I can't cry any more."

"I'm on duty, but I just had to come up and find out about Sally."

Sally's mother said, "The doctors found that the cancer has spread from the brain down into the lower parts of the spine, and that they could not remove it. It was too widespread."

"Oh," I said. "I am so sorry."

How inadequate I was. How ineffective.

And how selfish, in my inadequacy. I wanted so much to be able to reach out and help on this hard journey this dear woman, this darling child were on.

Sally's mother continued, "As soon as she recovers from the operation, in a few days we are going home. Later they may decide to give her cobalt treatment."

Then she added, "Do you remember my friend who was here?" I nodded.

"She was so upset after the operation when she found out what was causing the pain, making Sally act so wild at times. She felt just awful after she had said all those things about my disciplining Sally."

I said, "She didn't realize. Sometimes we don't realize what we say when we attempt to make value judgments on the actions of others. She didn't realize.

"But you were right. If Sally were well she never would have screamed at you and scratched you. She loves you too much. And you've both been through so much together.

"And," I added slowly, "I love you both so dearly you will just never know."

Sally's mother said, "I do know, Virginia. We feel that way about you. Sally is asleep now, and I know you have to go back on duty. But thank you so much for coming up. I'll keep in touch with you."

I turned and walked down the hallway. Numb again.

Catherine Collier.

This dear precious girl, Sally.

I went by way of the hospital gift shop and bought several kinds of get well cards. And also a small packet of festive balloons.

I wrote a note in a cheery card, and put the flat packet of brightly colored balloons in it. Then I placed the envelope in the mailbox at Information. Sally would have a hand-delivered note from me that very day.

As I walked down the hallway, returning to the Emergency Room, I thought, "I have been a Pink Lady volunteer in this hospital for only a few weeks. How can so many things have happened to tear into me with such shattering intensity. And I was feeling sorry for myself because my baby, my grown daughter had merely gone to another city to work."

I struggled through the day, and saw Ann Bennett just before leaving. I told her about how I felt so guilty for filling up with tears so often.

Ann said, "You have to get your feelings out in the open. Or else they really will tear you up."

I said, "I've got a lot of thinking to do. Maybe I'm really like that lady who said she could never work in the Emergency Room because she had too much sympathy for people. I'm turning into a sob sister and a bleeding heart. And that won't do. You can't function when you start

falling apart because of what happens to people. Somewhere I've got to discover and grab onto some rock-solid
truth and substance if I'm going to keep doing this kind of
volunteer work.''

I was tired, exhausted. I was crumbling emotionally.
Undoubtedly the stress made me susceptible for the next
morning I woke up with a sore throat which I struggled to
throw off before it turned into flu.

ELEVEN

I had spent several weeks in service already, and one might
have thought that I would feel a certain monotony about
being in the Emergency Room—the treadmill of chores
that I did, over and over, replenishing supplies, folding
sheets, running endless errands, meeting myself coming
and going, repeating the same actions.

The routine was monotonous. But not the air of expecta-
tion, and the feeling that here human beings were down to
the essentials. You could never tell what was going to
happen.

One of my more unusual encounters occurred one day
when I got involved in an unexpected discussion with a
young doctor. It was not the usual hospital conversation.

I was passing Room Nine where I saw a suture set-up. A
man lay on the stretcher bed, on his side.

101

An Intern came out of Room Nine as I passed, and said, "Good morning, Mrs. Greer. What are you writing now? Are you working on another book?"

Gracious! How did he know that I was a writer (a sometime writer)? Or even my name?

Daily a Pink Lady hears the interns' names called over the page, but I was not always able to put a face together with a name. The doctors, of course, related primarily to the nurses and not the volunteers.

Miss Sarazen came out of Room Ten and smiled as she came toward me. She had that dimpled smile and the quietest voice, soft as the fall of rain in a deep forest.

She said, "Good morning, Mrs. Greer. It's so good to see you."

She added, "Mrs. Greer, would you put a can of four by fours in Room Nine?"

"Yes, Ma'am," I said. "I'll be glad to. I was just going to check rooms for them."

"Good," she said.

I went into the large E.R. central supply room. I reached on to an upper shelf for a can of sterile gauze sponges, and carried it across the corridor into Room Nine. Warily, I skirted the suture set-up and placed the can on the table at the far side of the room where the sponges were kept.

The young intern walked into Room Nine. His complexion was ruddy. His hair was dark, close-cropped as a Marine, and he had a football player's build. There was something youthfully appealing about him.

The intern said to me, "Mrs. Greer, would you put some four by fours here on the suture table, please? Do you know how to do that?"

102

"Yes, doctor, I know how," I said quickly. I was quite proud of myself. I opened the squat can of four by fours, took the long forceps resting in the nearby tall can of Zephiran and gingerly grasped several sterile gauze sponges from the can and deposited them onto the suture set-up linen. All the while keeping them away from my clothes to avoid contamination.

Miss Scarbrough taught her girls well!

The doctor, who had not yet put on sterile gloves to begin his suturing, said, "Mrs. Greer, sure enough, what are you writing? You must be working on something."

"No, doctor, I'm doing a lot of thinking. But no writing right now."

Miss Scarbrough had given several copies of my first book, *Give Them Their Dignity*, to a few young interns. Perhaps he was one, and that's how he knew I wrote.

At that moment, Miss Sarazen walked back into Room Nine. "Are you ready for your gloves, Dr. Puzzel?"

Dr. Puzzel said, "Yes, thank you, Miss Sarazen." He held out his hand as Miss Sarazen picked up the sterile glove package waiting where she had placed it earlier, opening the paper container sufficiently for the doctor to remove the gloves in sterile condition. He put on one, then the other.

He said, "Mrs. Greer, you are a Christian, aren't you?"

The question was so unexpected. I said, "Why do you ask?"

"Well, you *are*, aren't you?"

I said, "Yes."

Suddenly he announced, "Miss Sarazen, I believe I'll get Mrs. Greer to assist me."

He said to me, "Mrs. Greer, do you know how to put on

sterile gloves?'' He wanted *me* to assist. Me? To assist a doctor in a sewing up operation.

"No, Doctor, I've never put on sterile gloves before. Is it permitted for me to put on gloves and assist?"

I think my words tumbled in a panicked flow.

He laughed a hearty laugh. "Miss Sarazen, will you help Mrs. Greer put on sterile gloves?"

"Yes I will, doctor," said that sweet voice of Miss Sarazen.

Then she did for me, what I had on occasion done for doctors when E. R. had been real busy. She opened a glove packet and held it up without touching the glove, for me to remove the glove and slip a hand in.

The doctor said, "Mrs. Greer, will you stand on that side so you can cut the sutures as I tie them?"

"Yes, doctor," I said as I moved to the far side of the stretcher bed.

Since I had on sterile gloves and was not to contaminate them, the doctor said, "Miss Sarazen, will you hold the Xylocaine for me, please."

It was only now that I really became aware of the patient. I realized it was a fairly minor suture job, otherwise the doctor would never have asked me to assist.

A tall man of about sixty years lay on his side on the bed. His left ear had a long gash on the backside clear down into the point where the ear joins the head. It had already been cleansed with antiseptic. He was dourly, silently awaiting the operation.

Miss Sarazen picked up the small bottle of Xylocaine, wiped the rubber-stoppered top with an alcohol-saturated cotton ball. Then holding the Xylocaine bottle upside

104

down, extended it toward the doctor. The doctor inserted a hypodermic needle through the rubber stopper, filled it then withdrew the needle in a quick movement.

Miss Sarazen smiled at me, gave me a nod of encouragement and said, ''Mrs. Greer, you'll do just fine.'' She left the room.

Dr. Puzzel said to the patient, ''This is going to hurt for a minute, then you won't feel a thing.'' The man said nothing.

He injected the ear along the line of the gash. Xylocaine was fast. It would take only a minute or two before the suturing area would be completely numb.

Then he lifted and gently placed a large square of sterile cloth with a hole in the center over the side of the patient's head. It was a ''sterile drape.'' His ear protruded through the center hole.

Dr. Puzzel picked up the curved sewing needle which resembled a sloppy-angled fish hook, and from alongside it on the suture table he lifted the dark suture thread. He inserted the tip of the thread in the needle eye.

He looked at me as he said, ''Mrs. Greer, you are a Christian. What do you really think of religion?''

I wanted to say, ''What religion are you, Dr. Puzzel? And what do *you* think of religion?''

Yet something stayed my lips. I felt that in his brash way, he was looking for a personal answer. But I really did not wish to enter into an impromptu argument about religion. Not above a suture operation!

For one thing, anyone who is a capable arguer can out-logic me. I'm more apt to retreat into silence and my own steadfast beliefs.

"Well, doctor, you have asked a hard question," I said finally. "I believe in God as our Creator, our Heavenly Father. I believe in Jesus Christ as God's Son who died for us and rose again. I believe in the Holy Spirit sent to comfort us. I guess that's a simple and fundamental creed.

"I also always go to church on Sunday, and I work with a group of young college students in a Sunday evening group before church because I think faith demands a community of care. I'm a Baptist.

"I listen to the minister's sermon and feel uplifted. So I guess you'd say that religion for me is also personal and inspires me to reflect on myself and my life. I read my Bible a lot.

"Generally I don't do a lot of talking about my faith. Maybe I should. But I guess I feel that whatever religion we have somehow ought to be in the way we live; it's not a matter of simply going to church. I guess you could say that the reason I'm here in the Emergency Room is because of my faith. I want to help."

He stood there at the end of the stretcher bed, and held the needle poised, ready to begin the slow closing of the gash.

I was immediately to his left, at the upper edge of the bedside trying to speak my mind well and to stay aware of the job at hand so I would not contaminate either the suture set-up or the sterile drape.

I said, "I feel my religion very deeply. It is important to me. It gives my life meaning. In an untheological way, that's my answer."

"Mrs. Greer," the doctor said, as almost imperceptibly he stood more erect, his needle and thread poised above the ear. "I am a Catholic. But I've given up the church." He flung out the words as though he were flinging down the gauntlet.

The keen point of the curved needle bit smoothly into the flesh of the ear. I almost started. It entered one side of the gash, across, and then through the other side. Then with another instrument he intricately maneuvered the thread into a small knot, pulling it secure, but not too tight.

I had seen interns doing this same procedure many times. It had seemed perfectly natural. But not now under these circumstances. Then he said:

"Mrs. Greer, will you take those small scissors on the suture table and cut the thread now?"

With trepidation I lifted the scissors, and reached over to clip the thread. I felt my hands shaking.

"Careful," he said gently. "Don't contaminate the drape."

I was more worried about cutting off the patient's ear.

I eased my body back just a bit to be sure my clothes did not touch. I clipped the thread.

"Oh," I said in dismay. "I cut the thread too long."

I believe the patient grunted.

I was really relieved I hadn't made another slash in his ear.

Dr. Puzzel said very kindly, "That's fine, Mrs. Greer. Next time you can cut it just a bit closer. But that's fine."

The patient was amazingly quiet throughout the whole ordeal—whether out of politeness or total fear I don't know.

The fluorescent fixture just overhead cast a brilliant, unglaring light over the small scene.

107

In my mind I had a picture of me in an operating room—everything still, hushed, the doctor saying, ''Scalpel, Mrs. Greer. Sponge, Mrs. Greer.'' I could hear the simulation of a heart monitoring machine going, ''Bleep . . . bleep . . .'' Would I save the day (and not incidentally the patient) by reminding the doctor, ''Doctor, you left a sponge in. Don't close yet . . .''

My mind was such a gawky repository of soap operas, pride and fearfulness. My real concern was on not clipping too close, and responding to Dr. Puzzel's curious bedside manner.

''If you've given up on the church,'' I asked, ''why do you say, 'I am a Catholic,' then, instead of I *was?*''

He seemed surprised and then proceeded smoothly with the suturing, ''I have been going to church, to mass, all my life. But I can't take it anymore. It doesn't add up. I go to church and I sit there and I look around me. And I see hypocrites. I'm a hypocrite myself, no different from the rest. But there we sit. And there are church laws that don't make sense to me. You shall not practice birth control. I'm a doctor. I see the necessity.''

His voice was hesitant, but not his fingers which led the needle-held instrument as the nylon filament played through. He tied the knot, paused, waited for me to clip.

''That's fine,'' he said.

''And I see all those people sitting there, those mothers and fathers, nowadays with one child or maybe two. When I was a boy the families were big, large Catholic families. Birth control wasn't dreamed of.''

He was searching with obvious sincerity. As a Baptist,

what could I say? Catholics and Baptists hold Christ as their center in God. Yet there are traditional hang-ups on all sides that disengage people from church, and alienate Christ-loving people from each other.

He said, "How can I sit there and listen to the priest and know that all of us are sinners, hypocrites? It doesn't make sense."

"I know what you mean," I murmured. "I go to church. I listen to the sermon. I sit there and feel that everyone of us is sitting there listening and thinking, 'The minister is right. He is talking straight to me and the person sitting next to me. He's really hitting that problem or sin on the head' . . . I have that problem, too, Dr. Puzzel." I felt helplessly that I was making small noises, that I was not hitting at the heart of his problem.

"And something else, Mrs. Greer. You know the Catholic Church has laws we are supposed to obey. There are certain sins that are mortal. That means if you commit them wilfully you are in danger of going to hell or purgatory.

"We used to be taught that if you ate the wrong food, meat on Friday that was a sin. All those years."

He stood back for me to clip. He shook his head as he did.

"Now, that's all changed. Rome has ruled that it is no longer a sin. We were taught absolutes, and now not only the rules but the game has changed. We're told that some things are not absolutes at all."

I clipped the thread, neat, not too close, but not long enough to look like part of a bow-tie.

He said, "Can you tell me this, what's happened to all those poor souls consigned to hell before the rules changed?"

Why had I come to the Emergency Room today? To stand over a silent patient with a slashed ear and enter into a dialogue on religion?

If ever an unsettling moment settled over a Pink Lady, it was settling down on me. I tried to weigh my words.

He moved his head slowly back and forth. "I don't get it. And I don't buy it. The very institution we are supposed to look to for guidance and trust, the church, changes its mind. I've given up religion."

He looked at me before his needle took its larger nip into the wider portion of the now-only-partly-gashed ear.

"I've got a lovely wife and a beautiful little daughter. And we are raising her with love and kindness and consideration as a human being. We are teaching her to love others and to live in a beautiful way with all people, as Christ taught.

"We love her and we are trying to raise her honestly and sincerely with love. But we are not taking her to church."

I was silent. He was tying the knot. I cut the suture thread.

"Dr. Puzzel," I finally said. "To raise your little girl with love is a fine thing. True, some people who take their children to church do not do that. People forget to live with lovingkindness in Christ-like love with their own children.

"But," I said, "Dr. Puzzel, she needs the church and the church needs her. Sure the church is imperfect — because the world is, and we are. But how can we be

110

Christians elsewhere if we can't be Christian in church. We all know that we love home and family even though we have conflicts in them. The church is our Christian home, a place of conflict perhaps, but a familiar place in a strange harsh world."

That was a long speech for me. Yet it had slipped out almost before I could form the words, because it was a subject on which I felt strongly.

"But I've got a problem, Mrs. Greer," said the young doctor, almost as if he hadn't heard me, his mind intent on his own thoughts. He was nearing the last few sutures. He asked me to hold the man's ear forward a bit as he worked toward closing the lower edge. The anesthetic may have begun to wear off, because for the first time our silent partner twitched a bit, and asked how much longer this was going to take.

"I'm completing my internship here at Mobile General. next summer I'm going into general practice."

"Doctor, that's wonderful," I said.

"I've got the offer of a practice in a small Mississippi town. And I want to take my wife and daughter there."

This came as a surprise to me: small Mississippi town. The doctor's accent was so obviously northern.

He caught my look. "My wife is from the South. I've come to love the South, and I want to stay down here."

He said, "But Mrs. Greer, when I take my family and set up practice in that small community, the first thing they'll ask is where I go to church. Then people will be after me to go to this church or that church."

Now I saw why it was so much on his mind. It was a

111

quandary for him as he began one of the significant steps in his life. He was entering private medical practice, uprooted religiously and geographically.

He made one of the last sutures, eased it to a conclusion. I clipped.

He said, "But I don't care what anyone says, Mrs. Greer. I am not going to church. I would be a bigger hypocrite than I am if I did." He completed the final suture and I cut the final knot. Then he removed the drape.

"Well a little prayer might help both y'all work a little faster," our patient said. He sat up on the table gingerly touching his ear. And we all burst into laughter.

"Maybe he's right," Dr. Puzzel said.

What could I say? Dr. Puzzel would have to find the way for himself. With the very compassion of Christ apparent in his concern for others, I felt, with a certainty hard to explain, that he would eventually find peace.

All I could say was, "Dr. Puzzel, you and your family *will* find your way to a church, I'm sure. Every time you lift your hands to serve your patients, you are joining hands with God. You are serving Christ."

Dr. Puzzel raised his head slowly. His smile turning serious, he gave me a long evaluating look.

Then he touched the man on the shoulder and said, "Thanks for hanging in there with us. We're all through. The nurse will put a bandage on, and you can go. Come back in a week and we'll take the stitches out."

Dr. Puzzel stepped back, peeled off his gloves, put a foot on the foot-pedal of the wastecan and dropped the gloves into the opened container.

He said, "And thank you for helping me, Mrs. Greer."

He walked from that room to other emergency patients. I pushed the suture table on its little roller feet back away from the stretcher bed. I poured the tiny container of tincture into the pan with the used sterile water-antiseptic solution, then poured the pink concoction carefully down the sink drain. I replaced the pan on the table, put all the suture instruments into it.

Then I lifted the corners of the cloth beneath the entire set-up and carried it to the "dirty room" at the rear of the Emergency Room. Only then did I take off and deposit my rubber gloves in a wastecan.

I hoped I had helped him. I prayed I had.

TWELVE

Sally had gone home once more, traveling that long hard route of illness between home and hospital. I mailed cards, and notes to her and always signed them, "Your Play Lady."

Then one morning, a couple of weeks later, Ann Bennett said to me, "Virginia, Sally is back in the hospital and her mother has been asking for you."

I hastened to the Pediatrics Floor and asked for Sally's room number. If she was back so soon her illness must have worsened. Hesitantly I pushed open the door of the room. She was in bed covered by a sheet. Her arms rested listlessly on top of it. A pillow apparently was beneath the curve of one knee, offering an easy cushion. More pillows were propped beneath her head, tilting her slightly upwards so she could watch television. She was very still.

114

Her lips appeared extremely red, her skin pale. I tiptoed into the room. Her mother was not there. I walked around by the side of her bed, smiling, "Hello, Sally," I said very softly. I patted her hand very lightly. "Do you remember me?"

Her eyes turned to me with an opaque stare. She appeared to be under sedation.

"I'm your Play Lady from the Emergency Room."

Her eyes lightened momentarily, a small weak twinkle in them. She smiled feebly. I knew she recognized me.

"Is your mother here?"

Her voice was faint. I had to lean down close to her lips to hear her mumble and whisper . . . "telephone."

"She's gone to the telephone?" I asked to be sure that's what she meant.

She barely nodded. I sat with her a while with the low monotonous tone of the television falling over us. Then I said that I'd go find her mother.

I patted her hand very lightly again. "You look so pretty, Sally. That's such a pretty housecoat." I spoke in quiet tones.

She smiled wanly, and I left her watching a cartoon. Her window ledge was filled with bright cards and flower arrangements.

I headed down the hallway and about halfway to the end I spotted Sally's mother at a pay phone.

She waved. As I drew near, she replaced the phone receiver. We opened our arms and enclosed each other. Then, we sat in the cushioned chairs in the corridor waiting room.

"I've been asking for you, Virginia," she said.

115

"Yes, I just learned that Sally was here. I was just with her. Tell me how things are."

Her eyes filled. She had always been so incredibly contained in the face of her heartbreaking circumstance. She blinked away the tears.

"The cancer has spread all over," she said. "They are giving her sedation to keep down the pain. And some parts of her are getting numb from the cancer. They say this is terminal but can't give any length of time.

"They won't do any more tests, because they don't want to put her through the pain. But I'm hoping she will get better enough to go home." Then she added, "We've moved to Florida."

I said, "You have both been on my mind and in my prayers. I've written to your old address, but maybe you didn't get the cards."

"Yes, Virginia, we did get them. They were forwarded to us. I just never was able to get a letter written to let you know how things were." She looked very dejected.

"I've decided that someday I want to write about my experiences here. Sally is so precious to me. I want to tell her story too." I added quickly, "But I won't use her real name. I'll call her Mary."

Sally's mother said, "No, Virginia, if you write, use her real name. I'd like you to."

Now my eyes were spilling over.

After a few moments of silence, she said, "You know, a doctor in New Orleans told me he wanted to write about Sally in a medical book he was working on. Maybe his book, your book will help others . . ."

And she continued, "The doctors here at Mobile Gen-

116

eral have expressed such a personal concern and feeling for Sally. They all talk about how she has touched them. A pediatrician here told me that she had become very special to him, too. And a visiting minister said that Sally's bravery has truly touched his life." She stopped, wiped her nose on a small handkerchief.

"Virginia, you know it has been hard for me all along. But now, some days I think I can't bear it. I have to keep my face and myself under control. It's hard.

"Sally has begun to talk of heaven. And she asks me about heaven. It's as though she understands and doesn't need to discuss her illness. When she asks me about heaven, I start to break down."

She fell silent. I could not say anything.

Then she said, "Use her real name. Let your story show a brave little girl."

Sally did rally sufficiently to return to their north Florida home. A couple of weeks later another letter came for me from her mother. It said, in part:

Sally is down to sixty pounds and bedfast. I really don't know how much longer I can go on seeing her suffer. But I do know this, God controls everything in our lives. And I know he gives me the strength I need every day. And I thank him for having Sally this long.

If I said that something went out of me when I learned that Sally was gone, I would not be telling the truth. For with Sally, something had come into my life that would never be lost. Something wonderful, rare, precious.

117

What had come into my life was a butterfly-borne miracle that touched my life briefly but left a memory draped across my life that will never fade.

We do not know the paths our lives will lead us along, the sudden catastrophes, the longsuffering endurances that we may face. We only know that we must take the suffering and make of it something beautiful that will fill others with the manifest awareness of Christ. Of God's love even in sorrow, grief, trial and despair.

A woman named Catherine Collier had touched me forever, as had all the others. A little girl with a brain tumor, in the middle of her own suffering looked at me and saw someone special, and so made me special. Sally's existence reminded me of Jesus' life and teachings. She suffered and she loved. Could I do less?

Sometimes it is only pain that makes us look about us and know that each person is someone special. Sometimes only tragedy makes us aware that each person is loved by God, our Sovereign Heavenly Father.

Our Heavenly Father knows the reality of our sufferings. For, his Son, our Savior, suffered. And died. Then rose again to be with us forever. The Emergency Room maid was right. God cares. And Jesus is never late. He's here to comfort us while we live; there to take us afterwards.

THIRTEEN

I did get sick. The flu I had been fighting for so long finally overcame my resistance.

It is eery what the mind will do when one is in the midst of fever. My entire body ached from the flu. My mind raced over the episodes of the last few weeks. I had contacted my doctor and was now taking the antibiotics and the medicine to ease the fever and headache. I called Ann Bennett and told her of my fever. After telling me to take care of myself, Ann said she would find a substitute for me.

Somewhere in the recesses of the convoluted territory behind my fevered brow, phrases and snatches flitted, lingered, went past, returned:

"Too much sympathy." "Jesus ain't never late." Catherine Collier. "Pray for me." Sally. "Are you the Play

Lady?'' Mr. Grant with his dogs. "I wish I had my Bible."
The little burned girl.

Rushing, crowding my mind, now separating with great
spaces between, the phrases, the memory of faces, of
voices, of eyes that pleaded with mine. Hurrying, then
halting to tarry with me.

And over and over, I hurled the indictment at myself,
"Too emotional, too emotional."

Finally, the fever was gone. And on the third day there
came a card for me in the mail. A beautiful metallic
copper-toned card with printed words to cheer the heart
with prayer, and then the note:

We miss you in E.R. Hurry back. We're running
out of sheets!

Signed by many hands. I sat there at home in a chair in
the late afternoon, holding the card in my hands, fingering
it, looking far away, then re-reading the words.

Perhaps I could help in some small way. Now, all the
faces and voices that had crowded my feverish mind came
back to me, but in quiet presentation of themselves and
their need.

Catherine Collier. God had been with her, drawing her
unto himself. She had fought a long hard fight. Tribula-
tion, abandonment, betrayal.

Our precious Lord Jesus had suffered all that. And
more.

And yet, Catherine Collier, as Paul in the Bible, had
fought the good fight, had run her course. We are all
human. Each with a certain span upon the earth.

And Mr. Grant. Whatever his path in the closing years

of his life led to, his Bible would sustain and comfort him, would give him strength from the Lord.

I kept thinking, in the midst of all the tragedies on this earth, God is sovereign. God is over all. He has a master plan. If we survive for a while longer, or if we die, we know that our Heavenly Father is sovereign, over this world and the next. And the sorrow each of us suffers can make us more caring. That is our human task and the task of the church.

In a strange and fulfillingly searching way I was trying to come to terms with all the sights and scenes and people whose lives had recently intersected mine, who had touched me with their being in the Emergency Room.

And I realized something else too. I was coming to terms with the departure of my daughter, our youngest, our baby-now-grown.

Is the youngest child the hardest one for the parents to let go? I had gone through the steps of grief with each one's departure. For a child leaving alters what is left behind. Mother and father finally find themselves merely man and wife once again. Separation brings sorrow. It can also bring new freedom to those left as well as those who leave.

That evening as I was recovering from the flu, our youngest daughter, Happy, called. Perhaps it is because the youngest child seems to be home for the longest, that a certain bond sometimes develops. A kind of sixth sense develops between youngest child and parents.

I had written her about my Pink Lady volunteer work. And now, she had called, just wanting to visit by phone. She was very interested in what I was doing.

I could remember when Happy had gone to first grade. She was six years old. A very wise and kind child. She had looked at me with her solemn brown eyes and said, "Mama, now that I'm going to school, I want you to have another baby so you won't get lonesome."

I had hugged her tightly even as I thought to myself, "Lonesome? Me? Old lonesome Jenny? Never!"

And now as we talked, my grown-up daughter and I, I shared with her my worst fears about my ability to serve and to stand the sorrow.

I told Happy about Sally, and about how I had just sat there with my arm about the woman whose husband had died of a heart attack, unable to say any words of comfort to her, just sat there and wept with her.

I told her of the Emergency Room maid, of how she had come into the small room, and of the words she had said. "Mary, call on Jesus to help. You call on him. Jesus ain't never late. He's always on time."

"Oh, Happy," I said to my daughter, "why couldn't I have said some words to comfort her. I feel them. But I just couldn't say them. I felt that I was such a failure."

There was a silence. And then my daughter said quietly to me, "Mother, don't let your ego get in the way. You were ministering to the woman in your way. And the Emergency Room maid was ministering in her way. And don't forget," said my wise young daughter in an even softer tone, "Jesus wept."

And somehow, with her words there came into my whole being a reconciliation with all that I had gone through, with all that I had experienced. I knew that even as I grieved for others, I was working through and easing my own grief.

We minister in whatever way we can. And as we grow, lives touch ours and our lives touch others. We grow in understanding and become more able to minister. The very suffering that we see in others, that we sometimes endure in our own lives, causes us to be more embracing, more comprehending and as a result, more helpful.

The woman who had said, "I have too much sympathy for people," had caused me to think greatly on this. I am too emotional, I kept telling myself.

And yet as I looked at the way I had reacted, had felt, had known torment of mind over the sufferings of these people, I knew that I did not want to quash my emotions and hold myself so firmly in control that I would not feel what is responsive and human in me. The sorrow I feel for another's pain is at the core of what is human in me.

I thanked Happy for her help and we said goodbye.

And part of the simple prayer of St. Francis of Assisi came to me:

Oh Divine Master, grant that I may
not so much seek
To be consoled . . . as to console,
To be understood . . . as to understand,
To be loved . . . as to love,
                    For
It is in giving . . . that we receive,
It is in pardoning, that we are pardoned,
It is in dying . . . that we are born to
                    eternal life.

Fear of my own emotions at the sufferings of others was not going to keep me from caring. I would go back to the hospital.

EPILOGUE

The years glide deceptively by, each day an eternity in itself. It is seldom that we reflect on a single day's contribution to our lives. But day by day our actions, relations and experiences are stored deep in our being. And one day, when we need an answer, if we have served man and God well, we will find the answer there within us.

My hospital experience was that for me—a procession of days during which my life intersected the lives of others. Reserves were being deposited by those who came into my life.

For eighteen months I served as an Emergency Room volunteer. Fighting my selfish fears, I slowly drew strength from the courage of others. They went beside me down the corridors of my days. Gradually I could smile more, weep less, all the while caring for patients with a deeper intensity than I had thought possible. The constancy of lives touching mine provided me an experiencing of life and death that no academic education could have offered.

Then one day, Ann Bennett's secretary had to give up her job. Her husband, a Presbyterian minister, was transferred to another city.

"I can substitute as your secretary, Ann," I said, "until

you can get another. There are so many volunteers now, the Emergency Room won't miss me. And I *can* type."

Ann said, "That's great. And you certainly know the complexities of the volunteer office."

The secretarial position was two-fold. The salary had been paid for, half by the volunteer auxiliary, and half by the Chaplaincy Council of the hospital, a volunteer ministerial program. Half of each day I would serve Ann's office needs, even a quick pinch-hit for a tardy Pink Lady, if she directed. The other half of each day I devoted to the chaplaincy program.

Ann Bennett had originally started the volunteer chaplaincy program under the direction of Rev. Jack Shearer, Methodist minister, and hospital administrator, Mr. Winston Whitfield. She gave me information and insight I needed.

Each morning (after putting the coffee pot in motion) I would go to Information. There I'd seat myself at the patients' file, list each patient's name on a 3-by-5 card, and note the cause for which each was being admitted. These cards were used by the chaplain of the day as he visited the wards. Prior to his calling, however, I would check with each patient to see if he or she would like a pastoral visit.

One morning Ann said to me, "There's no sense in my getting someone else. You know the job. And you should be paid. Say you'll take it."

I served as Ann Bennett's secretary for a year. "Temporarily," I told her. "Until you really find someone else."

I continued to serve as minister-patient liaison, and as the chaplains' secretary also. Coming to know the ministers of many denominations was a beautiful and meaningful experience.

126

I had the opportunity to sit in on the planning program which was to minister to the just completed Psychiatric Unit of the hospital. I wrote a complete summary of the plan and mailed one to each participating chaplain. Each would be specially integrated in this singular ministry.

Some hospitals will not permit chaplaincy visits to their mental patients. But the Mobile General program served the total person. And unless a private psychiatrist objected to pastoral calls (which was rare), the patients were blessed by chaplains' visiting. I prepared individual cards on these patients for the chaplains.

Ann Bennett's rapport with the ministers was beautiful. "My men of God," she called them. They soon made me feel at home in their circle, and more riches entered my life. I offered suggestions to chaplains regarding certain patients. Sometimes a woman can gain insight in brief encounters with patients which unexpectedly reveal a cry for help. There are so many despairing hearts in hospitals, needing specific words of cheer, of hope, of understanding. I always tried to be alert to see the needs and advise the chaplains.

As I came to know them more personally, I began to understand the real nature of priests and pastors as called-men, bringing God's touch to gentle souls lying there vulnerable to pain and victims of the monotonous time in the hospital.

Then suddenly I was hospitalized myself. I became a patient where I had served. Admission cause: FUO. Fever of undetermined origin. Get-well cards arrived. One from a volunteer Baptist chaplain, Rev. Charles Gaston, who

127

knew my sense of humor well, was signed, "Charlie Chaplain." As weakly feverish as I felt, when I read it I had to laugh out loud.

Twice more, within a two month period I was hospitalized. The fever was found to be caused by kidney stones.

In many ways it was easier being a patient than a hospital volunteer. When you're ill you draw into yourself; when you serve you are drawn out of yourself. Learning to do both had made my spirit strong.

Eventually the life-paths of Ann Bennett and Helen Scarbrough would take them to careers beyond Mobile General. And my path would eventually lead into the valley of the shadow of cancer.

But when that time came, I found my spiritual reserves full and my heart inspired by all the people whose lives of suffering and courage had contributed to mine in ways I did not realize until my own time of deep need arose.

I would share that Spirit-led strength in my book, *The Glory Woods*. And in writing I would try to pass along some of the spiritual resources which had been lying within me.

There are those whose lives seem to tug with immortality at the hem of the garments of our soul. And what they teach us, we in turn must pass on to others. Each in his own way.